TASTES OF NORTH AFRICA

SARAH WOODWARD

TASTES OF NORTH AFRICA

Recipes from Morocco to the Mediterranean

with food photography by Gus Filgate
and location photography by Alan Keohane and Sarah Woodward

KYLE CATHIE LIMITED

ACKNOWLEDGEMENTS

With grateful thanks to:

M Lamriki, Royal Air Maroc; M El Kasmi, Moroccan National Tourist Office; Aicha Lhamiani and her colleagues at the Centre de formation professionelle de cuisine marocaine, Rabat; Boufemaa Mars, La Mamounia; Jean-Pierre Hupin, Paris Jamaï; and, of course, everybody who invited me into their kitchens and kindly gave me their recipes.

Photographic acknowledgements: page 2, 27, 47, 129, Gus Filgate; 6, 11, 19, 26, 66, 67, 105, 128, Alan Keohane; 15, 18, 46, 104, 148, 149, Sarah Woodward.

Photograph on page 2 *orange salad with cinnamon* (see page 130).

Paperback first published in Great Britain in 2001 by
Kyle Cathie Limited
122 Arlington Road
London NW1 7HP

ISBN 1 85626 412 2

Text © 1998 Sarah Woodward
Food photography © 1998 Gus Filgate

First published 1998

Edited by Kate Oldfield
Copy edited by Janet Smy
Applemac design by Kit Johnson with Dorchester Typesetting Group
Typeset in Quorum Medium and Berling Roman
Stylist Penny Markham
Home economist Linda Tubby
Location photography © 1998 Alan Keohane and © 1998 Sarah Woodward
Production by Lorraine Baird

Sarah Woodward is hereby identified as the author of this work in accordance with Section 77 of the Copyright, Designs and Patents Act 1988

A CIP catalogue record for this title is available from the British Library

Colour reproduction by Chromagraphics (Overseas) PTE. Ltd, Singapore
Printed and bound in Singapore by Tien Wah Press (PTE) Ltd

CONTENTS

INTRODUCTION

'Where there are doorways or basins and pools then plant round about such trees as laurel, myrtle, cypress, pine, citron, jasmine, Seville orange, grapefruit, lime and cane-apple, for these never shed their leaves. And on the largest of these trees hang trellises and bowers for your pleasure, and by the same means you may shade pools of water so they remain cool.'

From the MOORISH CALENDAR, translated from the twelfth-century Book of Agriculture (*Kitab al Felaha*) by Yahya ibn al Awam

Imagine yourself in an enclosed courtyard in Córdoba. Despite the heat of the sun, you feel cool sitting in the shade of an orange tree. The air is heavy with the scent of jasmine. Before you is a marble fountain. The tinkle of the water ripples in your ears. All around the fountain are flowers and fruit trees. You nibble on a salted almond while you await your *ajo blanco*, an iced almond and garlic soup – the Caliph's precursor to gazpacho. Refreshed, you move on to *rape mozarabe*, monkfish in a saffron sauce studded with pinenuts and raisins. You may not realize it, but you are experiencing the sensual delights which the Moors brought to their beloved al-Andaluz over a thousand years ago. Pleasures which are reflected today not just in the architecture, and the gardens which were such an integral part of the Moorish style of building, but just as clearly in the food you eat.

If you find yourself eating grilled tuna on the west coast of Sicily, you might be surprised to know that it was the Arab invaders of the ninth century who first introduced the special nets to catch the fish. The techniques used are still followed today in the spring ritual of the *mattanza* at Favignana. If instead you eat *cuscusu*, couscous grains served with a rich fish sauce similar to that found over the water in Tunisia, you will have little doubt of the Arabic influence on the food. Finish with a cooling watermelon granita, the melon itself the fruit of the oases, turned to ice with snows from Mount Etna to make *sharb'ats*, the precursor to Italian ice-creams.

When you eat one of the sticky convent sweets for which Portugal and Spain are famous, you might remember that it was the invading Arabs who first introduced sugar-cane and thereby a love of sweetmeats. When the Moors were defeated, it was left to the nuns to take over the tradition of producing these almond laden confections, helped by the sherry producers of Jérez, who donated to the convents the egg yolks left over from the process of clarifying their wine with egg white. If in Provence you enjoy a pastry delicately scented with rose or orange flower water, then you should know that it was not the parfumiers of Grasse but the Arabs who first learnt to distil the essence of flowers from their petals.

It was the Moors who brought to the Southern Mediterranean the citrus fruits and almond trees which today are an integral part of the landscape. They developed the Roman irrigation system in the great valley of the Guadalquivir to allow the growing of spinach and aubergines. They drained the swamps around Lake Albufera so that there could be paddy fields for the rice they brought from India. It was the Moors who first grew croci for saffron on the plains around La Mancha and planted quince and pomegranate trees in the Generalife of the Alhambra, and many other gardens besides.

The word Moorish was used by the Europeans they invaded to mean a people from North Africa of mixed Arab and Berber descent. The cooking they brought with them was already as intermingled as the peoples. The signature dish of Maghrebi cuisine, couscous, was originally created by the Berbers, using the durum wheat introduced by the Carthaginians. The Arabs brought the spices with which the accompanying broth was scented, the Persian habit of combining meat and fruit for luxuriant stews and the rice from India which was to spread via their conquests in Spain and Italy into the rest of Europe. Just as Columbus was landing in the Americas and thereby starting a whole new food revolution, the Moors were forced from Granada, the last remnant of their once enormous and always beloved al-Andaluz. They brought back to Morocco in particular the culinary lessons the Iberian peninsula had taught them.

Today in Tangier and Tetuan, just over the straits of Gibraltar, there is a distinctive cuisine from al-Andaluz, an influence which stretched into the court cooking of Fez and further south to Marrakesh. The Ottomans were still to come, bringing with them new styles from the East, but these were to be incorporated into Moorish food rather than overwhelming it. So too for the products of the New World, particularly the tomato and the pepper, which soon crossed the straits from Andalucía.

The master cooks of the Moroccan court assimilated all these influences and ingredients to produce what the celebrated French chef Paul Bocuse has ranked as one of the great cuisines of the world. Among the interesting characteristics of Moroccan food today is the distinct similarity it bears to what we know of the food of medieval Britain's wealthy. They too enjoyed meat stews flavoured with almonds and honey, lamb with saffron and quince, chicken stuffed with semolina and raisins. And British medieval cooks used spices with as much surefootedness and care as one finds in the dishes of Morocco today, sometimes relying on an elaborate mixture, at other times using just one single spice to great effect, be that spice cinnamon or ginger, mace or cumin, even simply black pepper.

Moorish food then is not a precise cuisine, more a grand accumulation over the centuries of all that was best from different culinary traditions. There are distinctively Moorish foods in Spain and Sicily, Provence and Portugal just as there are in Morocco. But when dealing with recipes which in some cases originated in the eighth century few claims can be made to authenticity. Changes reflect the availability of ingredients, the tastes of the time, the very character of cooks who recorded their activities in the kitchen.

None of the recipes in this book make any claim to be historically 'correct'. Some are very ancient, others recent adaptations based on the Moorish tradition. Within Morocco itself there are many regional variations in recipes. A women from Marrakesh will always say that her cousin from say Rabat or Fez cannot prepare a particular dish *correctement* or properly – and vice versa. I have made subtle adjustments to some of the recipes in order that they may be simpler to prepare, without losing their essential flavours. If you want to change them slightly to your taste, feel free to do so. This is exactly how something as imprecise, and delicious, as the Moorish tradition of cooking has slowly developed over the centuries.

A LITTLE HISTORY

Sitting astride the main trade routes linking the Western Mediterranean and the vastness of sub-Saharan Africa, Morocco has seen many invaders come and go. The ancient Phoenicians set up trading colonies along its coastline. The Romans incorporated it within their empire as the province of Mauritania, developing its agriculture so that for a brief spell it became 'the granary of the Mediterranean world'. After the destruction of their temple in Jerusalem, many Jews emigrated there, as did Coptic Christians from Egypt. Then, as the Roman Empire began to fall apart, the Vandals swept in from across the Straits of Gibraltar. Further east, around what is now Tunisia, the Byzantines re-established control. But none of these were to have anything like the impact of a new force rising in the East – the Arabs and Islam.

Foreign rulers came and went… Yet the original inhabitants, the Berbers, have been living in Morocco's fertile plains and mountain fastnesses since the very dawn of history. Even today, the nomadic Berber tribes of the Rif, the Atlas, and the southern oases, retain a distinct cultural identity. The arrival of the Arabs in the seventh century, not long after the death of the Prophet Mohammed, brought with it the most significant change in their way of life, for the warlike Berber clans readily embraced Islam. The earliest centre of Arab influence grew up around Kairouan, in what is now Tunisia, from 670AD onwards. But only four years later the Berber leader, Kyslaya, converted to the Muslim faith, and by the end of the century all of North Africa was effectively under Arab rule. The Berbers remained, however, the majority population, and together with the Arab settlers in their midst, they soon began looking for new territories to conquer and bring within the *Bilad al-Islam*, the Muslim world.

The richest prospects for the Moors lay just across the Straits of Gibraltar, and in 711AD a Muslim army – led by Arabs but with a large contingent of Berbers – set out to conquer the Iberian peninsula. Their advance northward was rapid, and within the next couple of decades they had conquered practically all of Spain and Portugal. They also crossed over the Pyrenees, briefly establishing Moorish enclaves in the south and west of France. The tide was only turned back at Poitiers, where in 732 the Frankish King Charles Martel won a decisive victory, enabling him to push the Moors back behind the mountains or along the Mediterranean coastline.

The Muslims retired behind the Pyrenees, the front-line between Islam and Christendom stretching across the peninsula from Galicia to Catalonia. Meanwhile in 827 Saracen forces set sail from Tunisia to conquer Sicily. There was constant border warfare, from which grew such legends as El Cid, but the Moors were to remain in the southern half of Spain and Portugal for nearly five centuries. In the heartlands of Andalucía there developed a highly sophisticated Hispano-Moorish culture. Córdoba grew to be the most populous and cosmopolitan city in Europe, home to scientists and scholars such as Averroes (Ibn Rushid) and the main conduit through which knowledge of Aristotle and the ancient Greeks was transmitted to the 'barbarian' north.

Moorish Spain – or al-Andaluz, as it was then known – soon eclipsed the original Moorish heartlands of North Africa in terms of its wealth and sophistication. But throughout the Islamic period, links between the two remained very close. Indeed, for long periods southern Spain and Morocco formed part of the same empire. Thus, when Morocco's first Muslim dynasty, founded by Moulay Idriss, foundered, it was the rulers of al-Andaluz who stepped in to fill the power vacuum. These were the Ummayyad dynasty, descendants of the early caliphs who had ruled from Damascus, and for a brief period they brought both Spain and Morocco within a single empire, repulsing rival claimants from Tunisia. But their first priority was to defend al-Andaluz against the Christian *reconquista*, leaving the way open for takeover in North Africa by the Almovarides, a resurgent Berber tribe from the deserts of the deep south, who established their capital at Marrakesh. Initially, the Almovarides may have been less sophisticated than the Andalusians, but no one could deny their prowess in battle or the strength they drew from their closely-linked clans.

Over the following centuries a pattern emerges, of warlike and uncorrupted tribes sweeping in from the desert or high mountains, seizing power from the more urbanized and decadent elite, and then over time succumbing to the same softening influences of city life. The Almovarides were displaced by the Almohades from the High Atlas, who in turn lost control to the Merinides from the borderlands with what is now Algeria. And so it continues to the present day, King Hassan II tracing his ancestry back to tribal leaders from the oases of Tafilalt in the far south-east of the country.

Power struggles and internecine wars in North Africa reduced the flow of reinforcement to Muslim Spain, which by the late twelfth century was itself divided up among rival princes and coming under increasing military pressure form the Catholic Kings to the north. In 1212 came the definitive battle at Navas de Toloso, the pass to Jaén and the gateway to Andalucía and shortly afterwards the great Andalusian cities of Seville and Córdoba were lost, but the Muslim kingdom of Granada survived behind its mountain ramparts for nearly three hundred more years. Even as the end of their rule approached, the Nasrid rulers of Granada continued to embellish that wonder of Hispano-Moorish architecture, the palaces and gardens of the Alhambra. The last Muslim king of Granada, Boabdil, finally surrendered in 1492. Standing on a hill above his beloved city, on a spot ever since known as the Sigh of the Moor, he wept as he took one last look – provoking his unsympathetic mother to remark 'you weep like a woman for the kingdom you would not defend as a man'. Decades latter Boabdil was still being criticized – Charles V remarked, 'I would take the Alhambra as my grave rather than live without my kingdom in the Alpajurras.'

But the Alpajurras were in any case but a brief respite for Boabdil and the following year he fled to Fez, followed not just by other Moors but also many of the Jewish community. However some Moors did stay in the isolated mountains, creating beautiful orchards with their irrigation systems and building white villages in the style of the Berber homes of Morocco. They even plotted a rebellion in 1568, although this was rapidly crushed – with the help of the Moors of Mojácar, who had earlier sworn loyalty to the Catholic kings.

The last remaining Moors were ejected from Spain at the beginning of the seventeenth century by Philip III. But nearly eight centuries of Muslim presence had created a distinctive culture, and one which was ultimately to influence North Africa as much as much as it had southern Spain. For in al-Andaluz there occurred a rare fusion of different cultures – a mixture of the Arabs' love of water and the playing of fountains, their appreciation of song, poetry, perfumes and other sensuous pleasures, with the Mediterranean sense of voluptuousness and enjoyment of the land's natural abundance. Something of this was taken back to Morocco by Spanish-born Muslims who preferred to emigrate rather than to serve Christian rulers or abandon their faith – with the result that the loveliest gardens in Marrakesh or Rabat are described as being 'Andalusian'. And in Spain this spirit is expressed not only in Mozarabic architecture, in the gardens and orchards that flourish because of Arab techniques of irrigation, but also in the flamenco, the slow, studied pleasure taken in every detail of life, that is still the case in the blessed part of the world known as Andalucía. Its name is Arab, and so is its attitude – *alegría*.

SPICES

The Arabs, great seafarers and masters of the caravan trade, had long known the value of spices and quickly transmitted that appreciation to the peoples of North Africa. Together they took the knowledge of spice over the water into Spain. The Moorish invaders introduced to al-Andaluz many of the spices without which Mediterranean food is hard to imagine. Black pepper is just one example. It was perhaps because of the long Moorish influence that the Spanish court was prepared to send Christopher Columbus on his long journey to try to find a new route to the treasures of the east, never dreaming that he would stumble upon such different riches on the way.

In medieval times spices became almost equivalent to gold, certainly valuable enough to fight many wars over. The Moroccans, removed from Spain, nevertheless continued to trade across the straits and spices were one of the key treasures, brought across the deserts from Alexandria. Meanwhile in the court of Fez ever more prodigious use of spices was made to show off wealth – never more than with saffron.

Moroccan cooks today retain their love of spice and Morocco *souks* still feature spice merchants very similar to the apothecaries of the Middle Ages, selling herbal treatments and spice mixes for certain ailments. Many of them even have snake or animal skins pinned to the wall to be used in special mixtures and to ward off spirits.

Moorish food enjoys subtle spicing, whether from the complicated mix of sometimes over one hundred spices which goes into ras el hanout or the use of just one single spice. This is not cooking which relies on the bite of chilli, preferring instead a gentle underlay of spicy flavour. Cinnamon and ginger, cumin and nutmeg or mace are favourites in both savoury and sweet dishes, just as they were in our own medieval kitchens. Spices derived from the peppers of the New World were rapidly assimilated into the cuisine, and today paprika and cayenne are found in many dishes. The result is a delicate infusion of spice rather than an aggressive assault on the palate.

Right: ARTICHOKES AND ORANGES FOR SALE IN LA VUCCIARIA, PALERMO, SICILY

Black pepper

Pepper is one of the world's oldest spices, used by the Greeks and Romans as a medicine as well as a culinary spice. Brought from its origins on the Malabar coast in India, pepper was a great treasure which became known early on to the Arab sailors. The Moors introduced pepper to Spain and despite its expense it was widely used in the cuisine of al-Andaluz, perhaps as in medieval Britain as a means of disguising the smell of 'high' meat and as a preservative. In Moroccan cooking today pepper is still used in the old way, added as a spice at the beginning of cooking rather than as a final seasoning.

To enjoy its fragrance, pepper should always be kept in grains and crushed as and when needed.

Cayenne – hot pepper

The Spaniards had called black pepper *pimienta* and when they discovered hot chilli peppers in the New World they soon gave them the name of *piment*. Brought to Spain in 1514 as an ornamental plant, chilli pepper soon became used in cooking as a cheap replacement for the expensive original pepper, as it could lend dishes heat and bite if not subtlety. From Spain hot pepper travelled rapidly over to Morocco where today it has become an integral element of cooking.

The red pepper typically used is called *fefla de soudaniya* (from Sudan), although it originally came from South America – hence the English name chilli pepper, from Chile. The Marquis of Bute, in his wonderful book published in the 1950s, *Moorish Recipes*, remarks 'the red pepper has little taste and is used on account of its red colour, as cochineal is used in Europe'. I think he had simply been sold a bad batch.

Today hot pepper containing more chilli tends to be used, although it is still true that Moroccan food is not nearly as chilli hot as that of its Maghrebi neighbours, Tunisia or Algeria. The nearest substitute is what we know as cayenne pepper, again named after its source of origin.

Paprika – sweet pepper

Also derived from the peppers discovered in the New World, the best sweet pepper or paprika today comes from Hungary but a slightly less sweet version is widely grown in Spain and it is this which is usually found in Moroccan cooking. The quality of paprika should in theory be detected by its bright red colour but it is often embellished with colouring to hide its poor quality. The best quality paprika gives off a sweet smell and should be used particularly quickly.

Cardamom

The Moroccans occasionally flavour their coffee with cardamom in the Arabic and Turkish manner, but they are more likely to use orange flower water.

Cinnamon

The original spice brought along the so-called cinnamon route was cassia (which is still used in Morocco) and true cinnamon from Sri Lanka was first mentioned in the Torah then recorded by the Arab writer Kazwini in 1275. It was eagerly adopted by Arab cooks and Spanish cooks soon started adding it to the pot, particularly their lamb dishes.

You should have cinnamon in two forms – stick or bark, to be added whole to tagines and stews, and ground for both puddings and savoury dishes. In medieval fashion, ground cinnamon is still often used in Morocco with icing sugar to flavour savoury dishes such as *pastilla* and couscous *seffa*. Artistic cooks use the spice to draw geometric patterns on the finished dish. Of course cinnamon is also used in sweet dishes, particularly the most common pudding of *oranges à la cannelle*, and to dust sweet pastries.

Cloves

Cloves were widely used in al-Anduluz to pickle and flavour meat but today they rarely feature in Moroccan cooking, where their powerful flavour would overwhelm the delicate balance of spicing. However they are often used in Spain and Portugal for fruit preserved in sugar syrup and some Jewish versions of Moroccan preserved lemons include them for flavouring, along with a cinnamon stick.

Coriander

Coriander grows naturally in the Eastern Mediterranean. Mentioned by the Ancient Egyptians at the time of the Arabs it had become known as an aphrodisiac and was mentioned in the *One Thousand and One Nights*. While its seeds were used for pickling and flavouring meat, in al-Anduluz infusions made from fresh coriander leaves were added to a wide variety of dishes.

Coriander seeds have a sweet flavour with a hint of orange and are used mostly in tagines, particularly with vegetables. In Provence they are added to aubergines.

Cumin

Another native plant of the Eastern Mediterranean, cumin seeds have been found in some tombs of the Ancient Egyptian era. By the time of the Romans cumin was more widely used than the expensive pepper – although not necessarily preferred. It was a common feature of Moorish cooking by the time of the invasion of Spain and has remained a constant of Maghrebi dishes.

Cumin comes in seeds which should be toasted and ground. As with all spices, buy ready ground cumin in small quantities, keep it in a well-sealed jar and use quickly.

Ginger

Another ancient spice, ginger was the second favourite of the Romans after pepper and by the end of the first millennium its cultivation was well-established throughout Europe. It was used dried in medieval times as it is today in Moroccan cooking.

Nutmeg and mace

The nutmeg and mace, the lacy orange inner skin which surrounds the nut, were first discovered in the Spice Islands of Indonesia by Arab traders. Indeed it is to this that the nutmeg owes its name – it was believed to come from Muscat, where it was traded, and so became known as the *noix de muscade*. The perfume-loving Moors introduced nutmeg to Spain and must have appreciated it for its scent, which led in later years to the ladies and gentlemen of Europe carrying around nutmeg graters for when the smells of the street became too overpowering.

Although we may be more familiar with both spices in sweet dishes, in medieval times they were widely used in savoury dishes and are still added to some tagines. Both should be kept whole and grated or crushed when needed.

Saffron

The most highly-prized spice since classical times and before, by the tenth century saffron had been introduced by the Moors to Spain, which today remains the major producer, especially in the area around La Mancha. Indeed the Spanish word for saffron, *azafrán*, derives from the Arabic *za'faran* or yellow.

Brought back from al-Anduluz to the Moroccan mainland, saffron soon became an essential element of courtly cuisine. Its use was admired as much for pure extravagance as for the honeyed flavour and brilliant colour it lent to dishes. Saffron is grown today in Morocco in the area around Tinouit, but it remains very expensive and many Moroccan cooks use in its place food colouring or turmeric.

There has always been a tendency to falsify saffron and in the time of al-Anduluz spice merchants who tried to cheat their customers were severely punished. Today no such punishment exists for the spice merchants who sell supposed saffron to unsuspecting tourists in the *souks*, so it is wise to always buy saffron pistils rather than ready ground powder. For best results the pistils should be lightly toasted in a dry frying pan before use and then infused in a little warm water before being added to the dish. However when preparing tagines the saffron can be added straight to the cooking liquid.

Turmeric
Turmeric was traded by the Arabs and it is from them that it gains its name of *curcuma*. It always has been and still is widely used both in Spain and Morocco to give the correct hue to a dish in place of the vastly expensive saffron – in fact is sometimes called the 'saffron of India'.

Unfortunately with its colour it can also lend a slightly bitter taste, quite different from the honeyed sweetness of saffron. However, there are some dishes where it is essential, as in the Moroccan soup *harira*.

Ras el hanout
The mixture of spices known as the 'head of the shop' can vary from a simple combination of a few spices to one containing over one hundred different spices and dried herbs, with ingredients as diverse as dried rosebuds and Spanish fly – and has become the source of many myths. John Bute in *Moorish Recipes* claims it contains pepper, curry, cinnamon, bird's tongue, saffron wood and aubergine. Meanwhile in *Fès vue par sa cuisine*, another fascinating book from the 1950s written by a Frenchwoman who lived in Fez for many years, Mme Guinaudeau's suggested mixture is more complicated. Amongst the twenty-six spices she lists are monk's pepper (which she helpfully notes is an aphrodisiac), the rose of Damascus, cubebe, cyparacée (apparently a 'strong-smelling stalk from Sudan'), orris root ('found in the High Atlas mountains') and most worryingly of all belladonna berries – of which she notes 'very few are needed', which is just as well as this is the fruit of the deadly nightshade.

Spice shop holders today still make a great secret of their particular mix, claiming that it has medicinal as well as culinary powers – I have been told that *ras el hanout* will cure anything from stomach pains to infertility. The wise buy their *ras el hanout* as whole spices, to be ground as and when needed, thereby ensuring not just freshness but also a sneaky look at the ingredients. Best results are achieved in a pestle and mortar; épicier Mtibat Youssef in Essaouira told me with a look of sadness that 'these days I sell so much *ras el hanout* I have to pay my mother to grind it'.

Ras el hanout is particularly used for *mrouzia*, the very sweet lamb dish made at the *fête du mouton*, but can also be used all year round to flavour meat tagines.

HERBS

Fresh herbs are an integral element of the cooking process in Moorish food rather than simply a garnish. Bunches of herbs tied together with string are used to flavour the cooking liquid of a tagine; fish is marinated in the mixture of herbs and spices known as *chermoula*; very finely chopped herbs are used to add piquancy and fragrance to cooked and raw salads or are rubbed into the interior of a chicken before cooking. The biggest bunches of herbs of all in the *souk*, the market, are sweet mint, principally used to flavour tea but also sometimes found in cooked salads.

Celery leaves
The leaves from celery heads are sometimes used in the marinade for a fish and to flavour *harira*, the Ramadan soup.

Coriander
After parsley, the leaves and stems of coriander constitute the most widely used herb in Morocco – the two are often tied together in a bunch and used to scent tagines, the bunch being removed before serving. Today coriander is less often found in Spanish cooking but according to ancient manuscripts at the time of al-Andaluz coriander water, an infusion of the fresh herb, was added to many meat and fish recipes.

Fennel
The feathery fronds of fennel were traditionally used in fish dishes and go particularly well with sardines – as in tagine of sardines and the Sicilian *pasta con le sarde* , which was originally made with the wild ·fennel that covers the hillsides.

Mint
Mint in Morocco is mostly for tea but is also occasionally found in salads – it goes particularly well with orange salad. Over the water in Spain mint is often used in cooked vegetable dishes, for example with broad beans, especially in the Granada area. Infusions of mint were popular at the time of al-Andaluz.

Parsley
The parsley used is always the flat-leaved variety, known as French or Italian parsley, which has a sweeter and more delicate flavour than curly parsley. Almost all tagines have a bunch of parsley flavouring the cooking liquid.

Sage
Sage for centuries was regarded as a medicinal herb rather than a culinary one and still is mostly seen this way in Morocco. In Provence it is used as a flavouring for bread-thickened garlic soup.

Thyme
A herb called *za'atar* is used by the Berbers to flavour olive oil – the nearest equivalent to it is lemon thyme.

PERFUMES

The Arabs invented the process of distilling and it is from them that we get our word alcohol – *al'kahal*. In Moorish times the process was used not to produce spirits but to distil the essence of flowers into perfumes. The twelfth century *Kitab al Felaha* or Book of Agriculture contains several pages on the complicated process of producing rose-water, beginning 'Roses for preserving and distilling are best picked early, when rich in sap. If you pick them in April this is best…' and concluding 'rose-water of good quality should have a sweet taste and be a little astringent. You may also perfume your rose-water with sandal-wood, saffron, camphor, cloves or musk.' It is full of helpful hints – apparently if your rose-water becomes dark and acid you should mix in some of the edible mud dredged from the mines of Toledo ('which Abu Abdallah al Idrisi tells of in his book').

Rose-water
Little pink dried rosebuds are still found in every spice shop in Morocco and the ancient art of distilling rose petals to make rose-water is still practised today. The rose-water is used both for sensual pleasures – in a charming habit rose-water is sprinkled on the hands to refresh after a rich meal – and culinary purposes, particularly in pastries. A handful of dried rose petals is often added to a pot of mint tea to give a flowery fragrance.

Orange flower water
Distillations of orange flower blossom are used to scent salads in Morocco and are used in sweet pastries and puddings throughout the Mediterranean.

Jasmine water
In Sicily jasmine water is equally popular to add to puddings – it goes particularly well with watermelon in a granita.

FATS AND OILS

Traditionally Moroccan cooking features *smen*, a salted clarified butter which has a slightly rancid flavour and is kept for many months. In fact, the older the *smen* used the more honour you pay to your guest. *Smen* adds a unique character to a dish which is very much an acquired taste – and one which the younger generation often eschews. I use unsalted butter in place of *smen*, but the Indian ghee can also be a good halfway-house. There is also a trend to use more oil instead of butter. Morocco produces plenty of olive oil which may not be of extra virgin first cold pressing standard but is full and fruity. I particularly like the Berber oil scented with *za'atar* or wild mountain thyme.

Whether using butter or oil, fat is treated differently in the Moroccan kitchen from the Mediterranean style, particularly when preparing slow-cooked dishes such as tagines. Instead of using the fat to fry flavouring ingredients as a first stage of preparation, it is simply added directly to the pot together with the onion, garlic, spices and herbs. The butter or oil then combines with the water and flavouring agents to become a thick sauce. In the case of steamed or baked meats, butter or oil, again mixed with spices, is rubbed into the flesh before cooking.

The Mediterranean countries which the Moors invaded have always prided themselves on their olive oil and this remains their oil of choice.

MOROCCAN BREAD

Bread has a religious significance in Morocco – no meal is complete without it and the beggar's cry is, 'Give me bread in the name of Allah.'

You may wonder about the destination of the purposeful small boys you see weaving their way through the narrow streets of the *souks*, balancing on their heads wooden trays covered with cloth. They are headed for the communal oven, taking that day's loaves to be baked. Each family prepares their daily bread to their own special recipe, imprints their loaves with a special secret mark and then leaves it up to the baker to make sure they get the right tray back. No mean task when you are dealing with hundreds of loaves, and no small responsibility either. I once witnessed a spectacular screaming match when a fearsome elderly women accused an unfortunate baker in Fez of giving her back her neighbour's *khobz* – apparently a sin which would have the sure consequence of divorce when her husband tasted this inferior bread.

Khobz is often flavoured with aniseed or sesame seeds but the real secret of its flavour is from the wood-fired oven in which it is baked. This is sadly impossible to recreate at home so rather than trying to make your own bread I suggest you buy flat Arab style breads from the best baker you can find. As for Spanish bread – well, this is one area where the Moors did not leave a trace of their culinary magic.

SOUKS AND MARKETS

'It is spicy in the souks, and cool and colourful. The smell, always pleasant, changes gradually with the nature of the merchandise. There are no names or signs; there is no glass. Everything for sale is on display. You never know what things will cost; they are neither impaled with their prices, nor are the prices themselves fixed.'

So begins Elias Canetti in his wonderful essay 'The Souks', in the collection *The Voices of Marrakesh*. In his evocation of the *souks* he also draws immediate attention to probably the most powerful memory of western visitors to Morocco – the need to bargain. But if you have been scarred by this memory from buying pottery or carpets, forget it when you come to the food *souks*. Here it is not a question of price but of quality, freshness, even of source. A discussion of which *palmerie* a particular pile of dates comes from is perfectly in order. You are expected to sniff, to taste, to feel; in the end to bargain not for price but for quality. Everyone knows what each individual item of food should cost (and it is rarely much) – it is a question of which stallholder has the best on offer.

The best way to get to know the cooking of any country, of any city, is to visit its markets. The most remarkable *souk* in Morocco is in Fez – Fez el Bali, the old city as opposed to the upstart new city or Fez el J'did, built by the Merinides in the thirteenth century. No matter which gate you plunge through into Fez el Bali you find yourself in a tunnel vision of labyrinthine alleys leading to dead ends, steep hills up and down which mules and donkeys stagger bearing loads wide enough to plug the narrow streets, tiny squares roofed with netting through which the midday sun slants, vast doorways which promise of courtyards beyond but never open. As you are hustled along by the crowd, the noise, the all enveloping cloak of these dark and busy thoroughfares, you get a sense of the very medieval nature that Morocco still bears at its heart.

Fez el Bali is one big market, feeding upon itself. As one Fassi businessman told me, 'You can always tell a local – he creeps along the side of the main roads, turning down side streets whenever he can, so he can get his business done. It is only the visitors who walk in the middle of the road.' It takes days in Fez before you learn to look sideways rather than straight ahead. And then suddenly you find yourself in caverns off the main street, selecting spices from the sack, feeling grains of couscous, tasting olives from the barrel.

Back on the alley, you will find the fruit and vegetable seller who uses the iron chain suspended above his stall to him swing out of his little prison to help you select the best quinces or artichokes – or just to share a cup of tea, brought from a nearby stall by the small boy who also sells bunches of sweet mint. Food shopping can become a pleasantly long drawn-out affair.

Fez el Bali still has its Andalusian quarter, on the other side of the river above the stench of the tanneries. It is a very long way away from the prettified narrow streets of Granada or Córdoba. Until that is you visit those towns' centralized food markets, which for all their European hygiene regulations display the same fruit and vegetables, herbs and spices, the same passion for lamb as in Morocco. Move towards the coast and the atmosphere in the fish market in Cadiz is definitely North African – you can tell that the boats are trawling the same waters as those that deliver to Tangier. Swordfish and tuna, monkfish and sea bream, sardines and fresh anchovies – these are the most popular fish on both sides of the straits of Gibraltar.

You can prescribe a circle round the markets that ring the northern Mediterranean and find the same seasonal vegetables – artichokes, peas and broad beans in spring, aubergines, red onions, cucumbers, tomatoes and peppers in summer, pumpkins, cabbages and carrots in autumn. In all these countries the markets follow the seasons – and so does the cooking.

STYLE OF EATING

It is worth describing a shared meal in Morocco, because the style owes much to our medieval traditions. Whether you are in a palatial house, a small modern flat or even a troglodyte home in a mountain village, you will find a small low round table surrounded by benches padded with thick cushions. The luxuriousness of the cushions will vary and in rich homes you may find not just one table but two or three to cater for the extended family, but the principle remains the same.

The dishes are placed on the central table, often straight from the heat in the earthenware dish in which they were cooked, and everyone helps themselves from the same dish. There are napkins but no plates and traditionally no knifes and forks – although nowadays these are often produced to save westerners from embarrassment. If you are eating with your hands, use only the right one except for breaking bread. In wealthier homes a servant will come round both before and after the meal with a basin of water and a little perfume to wash the hands.

If the meal consists of salads and tagine, they will be served at the same time, the little bowls of spicy salads ringing the tagine dish so the diner can first pick at a piece of meat and then follow this with a spicy mouthful of salad. If however *pastilla* is being served as a starter (and this is a great honour for it is an expensive and time-consuming dish to prepare) it will be served quite on its own. The correct form is that after softly uttering the word *B'smillah* you plunge your hands into the centre of the pastry to pick out the choicest bits but be warned that this can lead you to burn your fingers – *pastilla* is served sizzling hot. On the matter of choice bits, it is customary for the host to pick out delectable morsels and hand them to their guests to eat. This particularly becomes the case as the meal progresses and your hosts will be aware that you are becoming full. And that is not surprising because tagines are usually served to guests in quantity. Sometimes, a couscous follows the tagines. You must try each dish but you are by no means expected to finish it, or even to make a serious dent in it. Hospitality means that the food is always presented in much larger quantities than the diners can be expected to deal with. Don't worry about waste – there will always be an eager crowd behind closed doors to finish off the leftovers. As the Marquess of Bute wrote in *Moorish Recipes*, "Long may such bounty last without restriction and without waste.'

A jug of water will be on the table during the meal but it is considered impolite to drink in quantity as this will fill up your stomach, thereby preventing you from doing justice to the food. A plate of fruit placed on the table signals the end of the meal, followed by a pot of mint tea or a jug of spicy coffee.

Of course this describes a meal for guests and does not reflect the habits of a typical family. But all Moroccan housewives are expected to cook well and many will still prepare lunch as well as supper everyday – not just for their husbands and children but for the extended family. Spending time in the kitchen is daily routine for the women of Morocco.

KITCHEN EQUIPMENT

No special equipment is needed to prepare Moorish food. But there are a few items which make life easier in the kitchen.

Tagine
This earthenware dish with the tall conical lid also gives its name to the slowly simmered stews for which Moroccan food is famed. A heavy cast iron casserole can easily be used instead of a tagine, although the combination of the earthenware material and the tagine's unique shape do lend to food a special flavour, especially when the tagine is used over a charcoal fire, as is traditional in Morocco.

Couscoussier
This is effectively a double boiler in which the aromatic liquid for the couscous simmers below whilst the grain steams above. It is also useful for steaming meats – but a conventional steamer does just as well.

Pestle and mortar
Although I use a food processor for many tasks, a pestle and mortar remain vital for grinding spices and crushing garlic and herbs.

Kebab skewers
Long metal skewers are useful for kebabs, especially if you are cooking over charcoal – dampened wooden skewers have a disconcerting habit of catching fire.

G'saa
A large round bowl of wood or earthenware, used for making the daily bread and for aerating the couscous grains. The important point is that whatever bowl you use for the purpose should be large.

A NOTE TO COOKS

All the recipes in this book serve 4 people unless otherwise stated.
I have given both metric and imperial measurements; when you follow the recipes please use one or the other but do not mix.

HOT AND COLD SOUPS

ABOVE: ALMONDS FOR SALE IN NARBONNE, PROVENCE. RIGHT: SELLING BREAD, MARRAKESH MEDINA.

Soups in medieval times were often one-pot meals, like Morocco's classic *harira*, the soup served at the sundown breaking of the Ramadan fast. *Harira* is traditionally thickened with yeast or fermented flour (although today plain flour and water is more typically used), a habit left over from the many yeast and bread soups which were popular in al-Andaluz. Many soups in Spain are also thickened with bread to make them more substantial – two good examples are the winter *sopa de almendras* (almond soup) and its summer iced version, *ajo blanco* (iced almond and garlic soup). Both these soups are based on a favourite Moorish ingredient, the almond.

As the call of the muezzin sounds across Marrakesh's Djmaa el Fna at the end of each day's fast during Ramadan, the crowds of hungry men who have been standing sniffing the air and waiting for this signal rush to the stall of their favourite *harira* seller. Taking their seat at the wooden benches, each diner's place marked by a small pile of dates, they watch eagerly as earthenware bowls are filled with the thick spicy soup ladled from a vast central cauldron.

Although it is particularly associated with the breaking of the Ramadan fast at sundown, this soup is eaten all the year round in Morocco – quite often for breakfast, served with honey-drenched cakes. *Harira* is believed to have its origin many centuries ago, in a nourishing semolina gruel which the Berber hill people prepared to warm them in the cold winters of the High Atlas. Over the years the recipe has been refined, with the addition first of spices, then with eggs in courtly circles and finally a reddening with tomatoes when they arrived from the New World.

RAMADAN SOUP

HARIRA

Harira *is best prepared in large quantities and is sufficiently substantial for supper. A few handfuls of broken vermicelli can be added at the last stage of cooking if wished.*

SERVES 6

175g (6oz) dried chickpeas, soaked overnight

1 chicken carcass or some lamb bones

1 large bunch fresh coriander

1 large bunch fresh flat-leaf parsley

2.5 litres (4½ pints) water

125g (4½oz) lentils

1 teaspoon turmeric

2 teaspoons ground cinnamon

1 teaspoon ground ginger

1 teaspoon ground cumin

1 teaspoon black pepper

1 teaspoon sea salt

500g (1lb) tomatoes, skinned and deseeded

2 mild onions, skinned and grated

2 tablespoons plain flour

150ml (5floz) cold water

2 lemons

2 tablespoons olive oil

12 dates

Drain the chickpeas and put in a large pan with the chicken carcass or lamb bones and the water. Chop 3 tablespoons each of coriander and parsley and reserve. Tie the rest of the herb bunches together. Bring pan to the boil, cover and simmer for 1 hour, until the chickpeas are soft. Remove the chicken carcass or bones and the herbs.

Add the lentils, spices and salt to the pan. Simmer, covered, for a further 20 minutes, then add the tomatoes and the grated onion. Simmer for a further 30 minutes.

Beat the flour into the cold water, making sure there are no lumps. Leave to stand; 15 minutes before serving, stir into the soup. Cook uncovered for 10 minutes, stirring. Squeeze the juice from 1 lemon, slice the other. Add the olive oil, lemon juice and the reserved herbs to the pan and simmer for 2 to 3 minutes. Serve each bowl with a slice of lemon dusted with ground cinnamon and a few dates.

GARLIC AND BREAD SOUP

ACCORDA ALENTEJANA

Garlic soups have been found all around the Mediterranean since Roman times and have long been the food of the peasants. I enjoyed this version, enriched with eggs and spiked with the coriander which the Moors taught the Portuguese to use, in a small dark tasca, surrounded by vast earthenware wine jars.

4 tablespoons olive oil

1 onion, peeled and finely chopped

6 fat cloves garlic, peeled

1 litre (1¾ pints) chicken stock

½ teaspoon sea salt

1 large handful fresh coriander, finely chopped

4 slices of day-old white country bread

1 tablespoon red wine vinegar

4 large eggs, very fresh

Black pepper

Heat half the olive oil in a heavy frying pan over a low heat and add the onion. While the onion is frying gently, chop two of the garlic cloves finely and after 5 minutes add to the pan. Cook for a further 15 minutes, stirring occasionally, until the onion is very soft.

Meanwhile preheat the oven to 150°C/300°F/gas mark 2 and put the chicken stock on to heat in a separate pan. Crush the remaining garlic with the salt and the coriander until you have a smooth green paste. Place the bread in a round earthenware dish in which it will just fit, pour over the remaining olive oil and place the dish in the preheated oven. Leave for 5 minutes.

When the chicken stock is just at the boil, add the vinegar. Turn down to a simmer and then carefully break in each egg. Remove the earthenware dish with the bread from the oven. Cook the eggs for 1 minute then lift them out with a slotted spoon, drain well and place on top of the bread. Return the dish to the oven.

ICED ALMOND AND GARLIC SOUP

Just as the Arabs brought the concept of water ices to Sicily, so they introduced to Andalucía the idea of iced soups. Ajo blanco is the precursor of gazpacho, milky white with almonds rather than red with tomatoes. Heavily laced with garlic, it is powerfully flavoured but deliciously refreshing on a hot day. Here are two versions, one from Málaga, the other from the Caballo Rojo restaurant, Córdoba.

AJO BLANCO

125g (4½oz) blanched almonds

3 slices slightly stale country white bread, crusts removed

4 cloves garlic, preferably new season's

4 tablespoons fruity extra virgin olive oil

1 litre (1¾pints) iced water

Sea salt

2 tablespoons white wine vinegar

1 small bunch of white grapes, peeled, halved and deseeded

Reserving four almonds, put the rest into the food processor along with the bread, garlic, olive oil, and half the water and process briefly. With the processor still on, keep adding water until you have the desired consistency – the soup should be smooth and not too thin. Add salt and vinegar to taste.

Chill for at least 1 hour – it should be ice cold when you serve it. Place an almond and a few grapes in each bowl.

AJO BLANCO CABALLO ROJO

400g (14oz) slightly stale white bread

50g (2oz) blanched whole almonds

2 cloves garlic, crushed

1 large free-range egg, beaten

Sea salt

White wine vinegar

Iced water

1 apple, peeled and finely chopped

Soak the bread and the almonds in water for 30 minutes, until they become soft. Strain them, squeeze the bread dry and put first the bread then the almonds through a mincer (you can also use a food processor but the bread will become sticky).

Beat the garlic and egg together and add the almonds and bread. Beat together until they become like a thick sauce. Now add salt and vinegar to taste and just enough iced water to produce a thick soup. Just before serving add the chopped apple.

MOROCCAN MINESTRONE

CHORBA

Serves 6.

250g (9oz) lamb or chicken on the bone

3 onions, peeled and grated

50g (2oz) butter

¼ teaspoon saffron strands

1 teaspoon ground ginger

1 teaspoon freshly ground black pepper

Sea salt

4 carrots

4 small turnips

4 small red-skinned potatoes

4 leeks

2 sticks celery, with leaves attached

1 large bunch of flat-leaf parsley

4 tomatoes

100g (4oz) vermicelli

Place the meat in a large heavy casserole with the onions, butter, spices and a good pinch of salt. Bring to the boil and leave to simmer for 30 minutes.

Meanwhile peel the carrots, turnips and potatoes and cut them into small dice. Finely chop the whites of the leeks, the celery including the leaves and the parsley leaves. Peel the tomatoes, remove the seeds and purée the flesh in the food processor.

Having simmered for 30 minutes, turn the heat up under the pot so that the soup simmers more actively and add the carrots, turnips, potatoes and chopped white of leek to the pot. Simmer for 5 minutes then add the tomato purée. Wait another 5 minutes before adding the celery and parsley. Cook for another 5 minutes, by which time the vegetables should be cooked, then bring to an active boil and add the vermicelli. Cook for a last 5 minutes and serve very hot.

CHICKEN, LEMON AND MINT SOUP

CANJA

The Arabs stayed longest in Portugal in the Algarve, where they planted lemon and almond groves, cultivated rice and instilled a fondness for mint. It is astounding what a difference that legacy makes to this simple chicken and rice broth.

1 chicken carcass, preferably with the wings still attached

2 litres (3½ pints) water

¾ teaspoon sea salt

1 large Spanish onion, finely chopped

125 g (4½ oz) white long grain rice

3 large juicy lemons

6 teaspoons finely chopped fresh mint

Place the chicken carcass in a heavy oval casserole in which it will just fit, pour over the water and add the salt. Place the casserole over a high heat and bring rapidly to the boil. Skim off the scum that will rise to the surface then turn down to a gentle simmer. Add the chopped onion, cover and leave for 30 minutes.

Add the rice to the pot, cover again and leave to simmer for a further 20 to 25 minutes, until the rice is very tender.

At this stage, you may like to leave the broth to cool, so that you can skim off the fat before reheating.

Before serving, remove the chicken carcass and reheat the broth. Place a teaspoon of the mint in the bottom of each of 6 large soup bowls, preferably earthenware. Ladle a generous portion of broth and rice into each bowl then squeeze the juice of half a lemon into each. Serve straight away.

VEGETABLES AND SALADS

MOROCCAN SOUKS *ARE FULL OF THE BRIGHT COLOURS AND SMELLS OF HERBS AND VEGETABLES.*

Wander through any *souk* in Morocco and you will find colourful arrays of vegetables, many of which are destined for the cooked salads which start the meal. Laden with spices, spiked with fresh herbs, scented with flower waters – with their exotic flavours from an earlier age these delicate appetizers set the tone of the dishes to come. They are often left on the table when the tagines are served so that diners can refresh their palate between mouthfuls of spiced meat, or even served at the same time.

There is no tradition of separate vegetable dishes in Morocco. If vegetables come with the meat, they will be cooked with it – the tagines and couscous broth often containing more vegetables than meat.

Salads are always offered as a selection, never as one individual dish. Icy cold raw salads such as grated carrot or cucumber sweetened with sugar and perfumed with orange flower water, or crisp lettuce mixed with segments of orange, are served alongside the cooked vegetable salads served warm or at room temperature and the spicy dips. All will be interspersed with colourful bowls of olives preserved with different spices and herbs and, of course, plenty of bread.

With their irrigation systems, the Moors introduced the *huertas* or market gardens to Spain, and today many of their favourite vegetables are cooked to be served as tapas to go with drinks – dishes like the Sevillian favourite of spinach with chickpeas or the Granada classic of artichokes with broad beans. Sicily, too, boasts many vegetables dishes based on Moorish habits, such as the sweet and sour aubergine dish known as *caponata*. All of these make excellent starters but can also stand alone as supper dishes.

BROAD BEAN DIP

BYESAR (BISSARA)

This is a popular family dish throughout Morocco and it is usually served as a hot dip, which is dressed with olive oil, cumin or salt before you dip in your khobz or flat bread. It can also be thinned down with water to make soup, which is served either hot or cold.

375g (13oz) dried broad beans, preferably without skins

4 cloves garlic, peeled

2 teaspoons whole cumin seeds

Extra virgin olive oil

Coarse sea salt

Cumin, cayenne pepper and dried thyme or *za'tar* (see page 18) to serve

Soak the beans overnight in plenty of water. The next day, if you have unpeeled beans, remove the wrinkled outer skins to reveal the creamy yellow beans below. Place the beans in a large heavy saucepan with the garlic and cumin seeds and add enough fresh water to just cover. On no account add salt at this stage. Bring to the boil, boil hard for 5 minutes, then reduce to a gentle simmer, cover and leave to cook for 1 hour, until the beans have broken up and are very tender. Liquidize with 4 tablespoons of olive and a teaspoon of salt. Sprinkle with spices and thyme before serving.

CARROT DIP

500g (1lb) carrots, scrubbed but not peeled

2 cloves garlic, peeled

2 tablespoons olive oil

2 teaspoons ground cinnamon

½ teaspoon ground ginger

¼ teaspoon cayenne pepper

½ teaspoon of sea salt

300ml (10floz) water

Place the whole carrots in a heavy pan with all the other ingredients. Bring to the boil and then simmer, covered, until the carrots are very tender. Process the contents of the pan to a smooth paste.

COURGETTE DIP

AJLOUKE DE COURGETTES

Tunisians are addicted to harissa, *the spicy red paste which they serve with couscous, and they often add it to their salads, giving them a characteristic red hue.* Harissa *can be bought in tubes and jars but you can also make your own (see recipe page 155). This courgette based dip is easy to make and the addition of garlic, spices and* harissa *gives it unexpected bite.*

1 kg (2 lb) courgettes
2 cloves garlic, peeled
Juice of ½ a lemon
½ teaspoon *harissa*
½ teaspoon ground cumin
½ teaspoon ground coriander
Sea salt
2 tablespoons olive oil
12 black olives

Bring 500 ml (17 fl oz) water to the boil. Peel the courgettes and remove their tops and bottoms. Cut the flesh into quarters. Boil the courgettes for 15 minutes, until they are tender. Drain and as soon as they are cool squeeze them to remove excess water.

Process the courgettes with the garlic, lemon juice, *harissa*, spices and salt to taste. Chill. Before serving pour over the olive oil and decorate with the olives.

AUBERGINE DIP

4 large aubergines, about 1.5 kg (3 lb)
4 tablespoons olive oil
4 cloves garlic, peeled and crushed
3 teaspoons paprika
1 teaspoon ground cumin
¼ teaspoon cayenne pepper
Sea salt
4 tablespoons finely chopped fresh flat-leaf parsley

Preheat the oven to 200°C/400°F/gas mark 6. Prick the aubergines with a fork and bake them in the oven for 30 minutes, until they are blackened and shrivelled. Leave to cool slightly then peel off all the blackened skin. Place the aubergine flesh in a sieve and press hard against it with a wooden spoon, squeezing out all the bitter juices.

In a heavy pan, gently heat the olive oil with the garlic for 5 minutes. Add the aubergine flesh, spices, a pinch of salt and half the parsley. Cook for 30 minutes, stirring regularly, until the aubergine flesh has become purée-like and darkened. Leave to cool and stir in the remaining parsley.

SWEET AND SOUR AUBERGINE SALAD

CAPONATA

I had cooked this Sicilian favourite many times before but according to Pirrera Gaetano I had made a fatal mistake. Pirrera is owner and head chef of the Ristorante Centrale in the medieval hill top town of Enna. Pirrera insisted that I must fry each of the vegetables separately. I must say Pirrera's version was delicious, if more time-consuming to prepare. The real key though to caponata is to get right the balance of sweet and sour that makes the dish.

750g (1½lb) aubergines

500g (1lb) courgettes

1 head of celery, including leaves

3 mild onions, peeled

Olive oil

750g (1½lb) ripe tomatoes, skinned

Sea salt

200ml (7floz) red wine vinegar

2 tablespoons white sugar

2 tablespoons capers, rinsed

2 tablespoons chopped fresh flat-leaf parsley

2 teaspoons chopped fresh oregano or marjoram

1 tablespoon torn fresh basil leaves

125g (4½oz) cracked, pitted green olives

Chop the aubergines across into slices 2.5cm (1in) thick and then each slice into quarters. Chop the courgettes across into 1cm (½in) slices and similarly the stalks of celery. Roughly chop the celery leaves and reserve. Cut the onions in half and then into fine half-moons.

Fill a heavy pan with olive oil to the depth of 1cm (½in). When the oil is very hot (it should be almost spitting or the aubergines will take up too much oil), add the aubergines and fry until browned on each side. Remove with a slotted spoon, drain on kitchen paper and do the same for the courgettes.

Now add the celery and onions to the pan, turn down the heat and fry gently until golden brown. Add the tomatoes, a good pinch of salt, the vinegar, sugar, capers, chopped celery leaves, the parsley, oregano or marjoram and basil, the olives, the cooked aubergines and courgettes and simmer until the tomatoes break down to form a sauce – about 15 minutes. Check the balance of sweet and sour and then leave to cool.

Caponata will keep for about 8 days (less in very hot weather) and improves with time. It should always be served at room temperature.

CONSERVED TOMATOES

TOMATES CONFITES

As if the sun-ripened tomatoes in Morocco were not sweet and tender enough, they are sometimes slow-cooked with sugar until they reach an almost melting consistency. This recipe comes from the famous Mammounia hotel in Marrakesh, where the cooking is courtly in style.

1 kg (2 lb) large tomatoes (they should not be too ripe)

1 teaspoon ground cinnamon

¼ teaspoon saffron filaments

150 g (5 oz) caster sugar

1 tablespoon orange flower water

2 tablespoons groundnut oil

100 g (4 oz) blanched whole almonds, fried in butter

Preheat the oven to 110°C/225°F/gas mark ¼. Peel the tomatoes, cut them in half across and remove the seeds. Place them on a baking tray and sprinkle over the cinnamon and saffron, the orange flower water and oil. Finally sprinkle over the sugar.

Place the tray in the bottom of the oven. Cook for 3 hours then leave to cool. Decorate with almonds.

SPINACH WITH RAISINS AND PINE NUTS

LES ÉPINARDS AUX RAISINS ET PIGNONS

This dish, of indisputably Arabic origins with its combination of fruit and nuts, is found from Portugal via Catalonia through to Provence, where it is usually served as a starter.

4 tablespoons raisins

1 kg (2 lb) fresh spinach

100 ml (3½ oz) extra virgin olive oil

1 clove garlic, finely chopped

4 tablespoons pine nuts

Sea salt and freshly ground black pepper

Soak the raisins in hot water while preparing the spinach. Wash the spinach well and remove any tough stalks. Bring to the boil a large pan of salted water and boil the spinach for 3 minutes. Drain the spinach, and refresh by placing immediately in a large bowl of cold water. Drain at once.

As soon as the spinach is cool, chop it roughly. Put the extra virgin olive oil in an earthenware dish over a very low heat. Add the garlic, pine nuts, drained raisins, the spinach and seasoning. Cook for 20 minutes, stirring occasionally. Allow the spinach to stand for 15 minutes before serving.

ARTICHOKE HEARTS WITH BROAD BEANS

CENTROS DE ALCAULILES CON HABAS

By happy coincidence, artichokes and broad beans are in season at the same time in the Mediterranean. I was shown how to cook this by a farmer's wife and this is her recipe, adjusted for the larger beans and artichokes we find in our shops.

2kg (4½lb) fresh broad beans in the pod

2 large artichokes

1 lemon

1 large onion, finely chopped

2 cloves garlic, finely chopped

3 tablespoons olive oil

A good pinch of saffron strands

½ teaspoon ground cumin

½ teaspoon paprika

Sea salt

2 tablespoons chopped fresh flat-leaf parsley

2 teaspoons chopped fresh mint

Pod the beans and blanch for 2 minutes in boiling salted water. Slip off the tough outer skins to reveal the vermilion green beans beneath. Set aside.

Now prepare the artichoke hearts. Cut off the stalks. Strip off the toughest outside leaves then bend back each leaf to break it off at its base. When you reach the soft purply inner leaves, lay the artichoke on its side and with a sharp knife cut across 4cm (1½in) from the base. Scrape out any hairy choke, rinse well and rub with the cut side of the lemon to prevent blackening. Repeat with the other artichoke.

Bring a large pan of salted water to the boil and boil the hearts for 8 to 10 minutes, until tender. Drain, cut into quarters and place in a bowl of cold water to which a squeeze of lemon juice has been added.

Heat the olive oil in a large heavy frying pan and add the onion and garlic. Fry over a medium heat for 10 minutes, stirring occasionally, until the onion is soft and golden. Meanwhile steep the saffron in 6 tablespoons of warm water.

Add the cumin, paprika and salt to taste to the onion then stir in the beans and quartered artichoke hearts. Pour in the saffron water and sprinkle in the herbs. Place over a low heat, cover and leave to cook for 15 to 20 minutes, until all the liquid has been absorbed. Leave to cool a little before serving with quarters of lemon and flat bread.

ARTICHOKES SICILIAN STYLE

CARCIOFI SICILIANA

Ideally this dish should be made with very small purple artichokes, but it also works very well with artichoke hearts.

8 large artichokes

Juice of 2 oranges

Juice of 1 lemon

2 tablespoons white wine vinegar

100ml (3½floz) of olive oil

Sea salt and freshly ground black pepper

1 tablespoon capers

8 anchovy fillets

Begin by preparing the artichoke hearts (see page 41). Mix together the fruit juices, vinegar and olive oil and pour this into a deep pan. Add the artichoke hearts, top up with sufficient water to just cover, and add salt and pepper to taste. Place over a moderate heat and cook uncovered until the hearts are tender – 10 to 15 minutes depending on their age.

When the hearts are cooked, arrange them in a serving dish and boil down the cooking juice to a syrupy consistency. Pour over the hearts, sprinkle over the capers, arrange an anchovy fillet over each heart and chill well before serving.

SPINACH WITH CHICKPEAS

TAPA DE ESPINACAS

This is a popular tapa in Seville. Breadcrumbs fried in olive oil with garlic are sometimes added, but I find it has a cleaner taste without the bread.

1 kg (2 lb) fresh spinach leaves

4 tablespoons olive oil

4 fat cloves garlic, peeled and finely chopped

1 teaspoon ground cumin

2 teaspoons paprika

½ teaspoon freshly ground black pepper

1 small dried red chilli

A few strands of saffron

½ teaspoon of coarse sea salt

1 tablespoon sherry or red wine vinegar

400 g (14 oz) can chickpeas

Put a large pan of water over a high heat. Wash the spinach leaves very thoroughly and when the water is boiling, plunge in the leaves. As soon as the water comes back to the boil, drain the spinach in a colander, pressing it down to squeeze out the remaining water.

Place a heavy pan over a moderate heat and add the oil and the garlic. When the garlic begins to sizzle, add the spices and cook, stirring, for 1 minute. Now add the spinach, salt, vinegar and drained chickpeas. Stir well together, turn the heat under the pan to low, cover and leave to cook for 20 minutes, stirring once halfway through. Serve tepid or cold.

EGG AND POTATO OMELETTE

CUAJADA

This omelette bears a strong resemblance to the Spanish tortilla. In Tangier it is still known by its Spanish name, cuajada *or filled.*

750g (1½lb) floury potatoes, red-skinned are best

½ teaspoon salt

1 teaspoon freshly ground black pepper

¼ teaspoon turmeric

A pinch of nutmeg

4 tablespoons finely chopped fresh flat-leaf parsley

6 large eggs

Olive oil

Preheat the oven to 200°C / 400°F / gas mark 6. Bring a large pan of water to the boil and boil the potatoes in their skins until they are soft – about 30 minutes, depending on size. Resist the temptation to prick them with a fork or they will become soggy – instead pick one out of the water and squeeze it in a cloth to see if it is soft.

Drain the potatoes very well and as soon as they are cool enough to handle peel off the skins. Mash the peeled potato with the salt and pepper. When the mash is very smooth stir in the turmeric, nutmeg and the chopped parsley. Beat the eggs and add them to the potato mixture.

Place a deep sided round earthenware dish over the heat and pour in enough olive oil to cover the base to a depth of 1 cm (½in). When the oil is hot but not spitting, add the potato and egg mixture, spreading it around the dish. Cook over direct heat for 5 minutes then transfer to the preheated oven. Cook for 45 minutes, until the mixture has slightly risen and browned on top. Drain off the excess oil before serving.

AUBERGINE SALAD

ZA'ALOUK

The aubergine has long been regarded as the king of vegetables in the Arab world and it was one of the first vegetables the Moors introduced to Andalucia. Despite that, it was many centuries before the people of the Mediterranean adopted the aubergine as their own. I can't remember ever having been served a selection of salads in Morocco without finding at least one aubergine dish.

500g (1 lb) aubergine

Sea salt

Olive oil for frying

3 fat cloves garlic, finely chopped

2 teaspoons paprika

¼ teaspoon cayenne pepper

1 teaspoon ground cumin

Juice of 1 lemon

Freshly ground black pepper

2 tablespoons finely chopped fresh coriander

¼ of a preserved lemon, rinsed and cut into thin strips (optional)

Slice the aubergine into rounds about 2 cm (¾ in) thick. Sprinkle generously with salt and leave to drain in a colander for 30 minutes. Rinse well and pat dry.

Pour olive oil into a heavy frying pan to a depth of 1 cm (½ in). When the oil is hot, fry the aubergine slices in batches – take care not to overcrowd the pan. When the slices are golden brown on each side, remove them from the oil and drain on kitchen paper. When you have finished frying, discard the oil and wipe the pan clean.

When the aubergine slices are cool enough to handle, roughly chop them. Mix in the garlic and spices and then return the aubergine mixture to the pan. Cook over a gentle heat, stirring occasionally, until all the liquid evaporates.

Add the juice of a lemon, a few grinds of black pepper, and salt only if necessary. Leave to cool – the salad is best served warm or at room temperature, never straight from the fridge. Just before serving stir in the coriander and decorate with the strips of preserved lemon if available.

TWO CARROT SALADS

Salads served as starters in a Moroccan kitchen come in different guises – a salad composed of raw vegetables; a cooked salad, served cold; and a purée of cooked vegetables, served as a dip (see recipes page 36–7). Here are raw and cooked ways of treating the humble carrot.

RAW CARROT SALAD

500g (1lb) large carrots

3 oranges

4 teaspoons orange flower water

4 teaspoons caster sugar

Juice of 1 lemon

Sea salt

Ground cinnamon

Peel the carrots, remove the tough core then grate them finely. Peel the oranges and cut the flesh into small pieces, making sure you catch the juices. Mix the orange flesh and juice into the grated carrot together with the orange flower water, sugar, lemon juice and plenty of salt. Sprinkle ground cinnamon over the surface and chill well before serving.

COOKED CARROT SALAD

500g (1lb) carrots, peeled and cut into batons

2 fat cloves garlic, peeled

4 teaspoons white sugar

1 teaspoon ground cinnamon

½ teaspoon ground cumin

2 teaspoons paprika

¼ teaspoon cayenne pepper

½ teaspoon coarse sea salt

3 tablespoons olive oil

1 tablespoon finely chopped fresh flat-leaf parsley

Place the carrots in a large pan and add sufficient water to cover by 1 cm. Add the whole cloves of garlic, the sugar, spices, salt and oil. Simmer for 15 minutes or until the carrots are just tender all the way through (test with a skewer). Leave to cool in the liquid.

To serve, discard the garlic, remove the carrots from the cooking liquid with a slotted spoon and garnish with the parsley.

CUCUMBER SALAD

Moroccans often use sugar in their salads, especially when combined with the perfume of orange flower water and the juices of citrus fruits – just as in medieval times. Far from being sickly sweet, when well-chilled the salads are very refreshing, particularly as no oil is used in their dressing.

2 cucumbers, about 750g (1½ lb)

Sea salt

Juice of 1 orange

Juice of ½ a lemon

4 teaspoons orange flower water

4 teaspoons caster sugar

½ teaspoon ground cinnamon

Peel the cucumbers and grate the flesh finely. Place in a colander, sprinkle generously with salt and leave to drain for 10 minutes. Squeeze dry with your hands. Mix together the orange and lemon juices, the orange flower water and the sugar and pour over the grated cucumber. Sprinkle over the cinnamon and chill very thoroughly before serving.

BEETROOT SALAD WITH CINNAMON

Although this salad can be made with ready-cooked, vacuum-packed beetroot (although emphatically not those preserved in malt vinegar), for best results it is best to boil your own beetroot. If they are dressed when warm they absorb the flavours much more readily.

750g (1½lb) whole beetroot in their skins

Sea salt

1 tablespoon caster sugar

1 teaspoon ground cinnamon

1 tablespoon orange flower water

1 orange

Scrub the beetroot well. Bring a large pan of salted water to the boil and boil the beetroot until they are tender – this will take about 20 to 30 minutes. Retain 2 tablespoons of the cooking water. Refresh the cooked beetroot in cold water and peel them. Either grate or dice the flesh. Mix the sugar into the retained cooking water to dissolve it then add the cinnamon and orange flower water. Pour this mixture over the beetroot and chill well. Decorate with slices of orange before serving.

LETTUCE AND ORANGE SALAD

2 Little Gem lettuces or other small, crisp lettuce

3 oranges

Juice of 1 lemon

2 teaspoons orange flower water

2 teaspoons caster sugar

1 tablespoon of olive oil

Ground cinnamon

Wash and dry the lettuces and roughly tear the leaves. Peel 2 oranges, cut the flesh into bite sized pieces and mix into the lettuce. Juice the third orange and mix with the lemon juice, orange flower water, sugar and oil. Pour this dressing over the lettuce and orange mixture and chill well. Just before serving dust with ground cinnamon.

See photograph on page 47.

RADISH SALAD

For this dish you need the long mild-tasting radishes rather than the round ones which are most often on sale. It works well with long white as well as red radishes – both can be found in ethnic shops.

4 long radishes

2 oranges

1 lemon

2 tablespoons of orange flower water

2 tablespoons of caster sugar

Sea salt

Peel the radishes and put them in iced water. Peel the oranges and cut the flesh into small segments. Mix together the lemon juice, orange flower water, sugar and salt to taste. Finely grate the flesh of the radishes and mix in the orange segments and the dressing. Chill briefly before serving.

MARINATED COURGETTES
COURGETTES CHERMOULA

Chermoula, *a fragrant mixture of herbs and spices, is most typically used as a marinade for fish (see page 56), but it also works well with lightly cooked vegetables, when lemon juice instead of vinegar is used in the mixture. Carrots also work well with* chermoula.

1 kg (2 lb) courgettes

Sea salt

2 cloves garlic, peeled

4 tablespoons extra virgin olive oil

1 tablespoon white wine vinegar

2 teaspoons paprika

2 teaspoons ground cumin

¼ teaspoon cayenne pepper

4 tablespoons finely chopped fresh coriander

1 preserved lemon, cut into strips

Cut the courgettes into 4 pieces lengthways then cut each piece across. Fill a large pan with water, add a teaspoon of salt and bring to the boil. Cook the courgette pieces for three minutes then drain, discarding the garlic. Mix together the remaining ingredients and pour over the courgette pieces while they are still warm. Leave to marinate for 24 hours before serving decorated with strips of preserved lemon (optional).

See photograph on page 47.

TURNIP SALAD

This is a salad to serve when the young turnips gently blushed with pink are in season. Turnips may be served raw but in this salad from Tunisia they are lightly cooked before being dressed.

500 g (1 lb) young turnips

Salt

1 tablespoon orange flower water

3 tablespoons extra virgin olive oil

1 teaspoon toasted cumin seeds

1 tablespoon chopped fresh flat-leaf parsley

Peel the turnips, remove the stalk. Slice finely. Bring a pan of salted water to the boil and boil the turnip slices until just tender – the exact time will depend upon their age and will be between 3 to 5 minutes.

Dress the drained turnip slices with the orange flower water, oil, cumin and some salt while still hot. Leave to stand for at least 1 hour before serving sprinkled with parsley.

LEMON AND OLIVE SALAD

This sharp salad is good as a starter with a selection of other salads and goes very well with grilled or fried fish. It is important to use sweet violet olives rather than the sharper green ones. If you like you can also add a finely chopped red onion to add extra sweetness.

3 very ripe lemons

Sea salt

1 teaspoon of paprika

1 teaspoon of ground cumin

A pinch of cayenne pepper

½ teaspoon of sugar

4 tablespoons chopped fresh flat-leaf parsley

4 tablespoons extra virgin olive oil

24 black or violet olives

Peel the lemons and soak them for one hour in heavily salted water. Drain and dice the flesh finely. Mix in the spices, sugar, parsley and finally the olive oil. Chill well before serving sprinkled with the olives.

SALAD OF ORANGES AND OLIVES

This Sicilian salad is indisputably of Arabic origin, which is fair as the Arabs first planted the famous Sicilian citrus fruit groves. In fact the first oranges introduced were the bitter variety which became known as the Seville orange – it was several centuries later that the Crusaders, returning from the Near East, brought the sweeter orange to Sicily.

6 oranges

4 tablespoons extra virgin olive oil

Sea salt and freshly ground black pepper

24 black olives

Peel the oranges and slice them finely across. Dress with the olive oil and plenty of salt and pepper, scatter over the olives and chill well before serving.

BROAD BEANS WITH CORIANDER

FAVAS COM COENTRO

Coriander is widely used in Moroccan cooking but is rarely found in the kitchens of Western Europe – except that is in Portugal, where it finds its way into all sorts of dishes. It goes especially well with broad beans – serve this as a starter or with plain grilled meat.

2 kg (4½ lb) broad beans in the pod

3 tablespoons olive oil

1 onion, peeled and finely chopped

2 cloves garlic, peeled and finely chopped

250 ml (8 fl oz) water

Salt and freshly ground black pepper

4 tablespoons finely chopped fresh coriander

Pod the beans. Heat the oil in a heavy pan over a medium heat and fry the onion and garlic for 15 minutes, stirring occasionally, until the onion is golden. Add the beans, turn to coat in the oil, then add the water and plenty of salt and pepper. Bring to a simmer, turn the heat to low, cover and leave to cook for 10 to 15 minutes, until the beans are tender and almost all the water absorbed. Stir in the coriander and serve hot.

MOROCCAN BROAD BEAN SALAD

3 cloves garlic, peeled

Sea salt

2 kg (4½ lb) broad beans in the pod

4 tablespoons olive oil

Juice of ½ a lemon

2 teaspoons paprika

1 teaspoon ground cumin

¼ teaspoon cayenne pepper

2 tablespoons finely chopped fresh coriander

1 preserved lemon

12 black olives

Put a large pan of water over the heat, with 1 garlic clove and 1 teaspoon of salt. Pod the beans and when the water is boiling add them for 2 minutes. Drain and discard the garlic. When the beans are cool enough to handle, slip off the white outer skin, revealing the bright green beans beneath.

Put the beans in a heavy pot over a low heat and add the oil, lemon juice, spices, a pinch of salt and the remaining garlic, finely chopped. Cook for 10 minutes, stirring regularly. Take off the heat and when cool stir in the chopped coriander. Decorate with strips of preserved lemon and the olives before serving.

TOMATOES AND PEPPERS

Sweet peppers, hot chillies and tomatoes: – vegetables that Colombus found in the New World and sent across the Atlantic – became an integral element of Moroccan cooking. There is some similarity between these salads and the gazpacho of Andalucía – but the Moroccan salads lack the sharp tang of vinegar which characterizes gazpacho.

COOKED TOMATO AND PEPPER SALAD

1 kg (2 lb) tomatoes, peeled, deseeded and quartered

4 green peppers

2 cloves garlic, peeled and crushed

2 teaspoons paprika

1 teaspoon ground cumin

¼ teaspoon cayenne pepper

4 tablespoons olive oil

Coarse sea salt

8 black olives

Put the peppers under a grill at maximum heat until the skins are blackened all over. Peel, remove the seeds and cut the flesh into thin strips. Cook the tomatoes over a moderate heat with the garlic cloves, the spices, olive oil and salt, stirring regularly, until the tomatoes have completely broken down – about 30 minutes. Remove the garlic cloves, add the pepper and cook over a moderate heat for a further 10 minutes. Remove from the heat and leave to cool completely before serving decorated with the olives.

RAW TOMATO AND PEPPER SALAD

4 green peppers

1 kg (1 lb) tomatoes, peeled, deseeded

4 tablespoons olive oil

Juice of ½ a lemon

½ teaspoon ground cumin

¼ teaspoon paprika

¼ teaspoon cayenne pepper

¼ teaspoon black pepper

½ teaspoon of coarse sea salt

3 tablespoons flat-leaf parsley

1 preserved lemon (optional)

Put the grill on its hottest setting and grill the peppers until their skin is blackened all over. Peel, remove the seeds and finely chop the flesh of the peppers.

Finely chop the tomato flesh and mix with the peppers. Beat the olive oil into the lemon juice then add the spices and salt. Pour over the salad and leave to stand for at least 1 hour. Before serving stir in the finely chopped parsley and the preserved lemon cut into thin strips.

FISH
FROM
THE SEA

*ABOVE: ANCHOVIES
COOKING IN TANGIER.
RIGHT: A BOWL OF FRESHLY
CAUGHT SARDINES.*

Although the enthusiasm for meat has sometimes meant that fish takes second best, fish from both the rivers and the sea has always been an important ingredient in Moorish cooking – especially in Morocco's coastal ports from Essaouira to Tangier. Little fishes, such as anchovies, are dipped in spicy semolina flour and deep-fried in olive oil for street food or baked in a spicy tomato sauce for a tagine; whole river fish might be stuffed with fruit and baked; sea fish are often marinated in the paste of herbs, garlic, spices, lemon juice and olive oil known in Morocco as *chermoula*; boned sardines are packed with nuts and raisins or cooked with saffron and wild greens in tagines and pasta dishes; and all sorts of mixtures of fish and shellfish find their way into the seafood soups and stews which accompany couscous.

In general shellfish is not often eaten in Morocco, except for prawns. But over the water in Andalusia and Portugal, where fish has always been the king and every imaginable kind of shellfish is consumed, Moorish spicing adds piquancy to many fish dishes. And the classic Sicilian dish of *sarde a beccaficco* is believed to have a long history tracing back to the Arab invasion.

Prized fish in Morocco include the expensive sea bass, the cheaper and more common grey mullet and the exquisite red mullet. Perhaps the most commonly found larger fish are *pageot* and *daurade*, varieties of sea bream. Sardines and fresh anchovies are consumed in vast quantities. Tuna, swordfish and shark are widely caught but quite often exported, particularly to the ever-hungry Spanish markets, where monkfish is also very popular. Shad is now difficult to find but used to be commonly cooked.

Moroccans tend to like their fish somewhat overcooked – I have slightly adjusted traditional recipes to take this into account.

CHERMOULA

No Moroccan cook could imagine fish without *chermoula*, the marinade of herbs and spices and garlic, all mixed with lemon juice and olive oil, with which it is almost always prepared and which is for me one of the trademarks of Moroccan cuisine. When used as a marinade *chermoula* should be pounded in a pestle and mortar or processed with a little water to make a slightly crunchy paste, but I also like it more roughly chopped as a cold sauce for fried fish.

Here are three recipes from three different people in three different cities – there are endless permutations and regional variations. From my point of view they are all good – the point is to marinate the fish to give it fragrance and as long as the balance is right then it will taste correct. Taste to experiment, but do not add onion when marinating fish for the grill or the tagine – it will overwhelm rather than add.

CHERMOULA 1

A RECIPE FROM TANGIER

This recipe comes from the Ristorante Valencia in Tangier. Hidden away up a side street from the sea-front, it serves incredibly fresh fish and its Spanish chef recognizes the value of the chermoula *marinade – though his version is without cumin or fresh coriander.*

3 cloves garlic, peeled

½ teaspoon coarse sea salt

4 tablespoons finely chopped fresh parsley

4 tablespoons extra virgin olive oil

Juice of ½ a lemon

2 teaspoons paprika

¼ teaspoon cayenne pepper

½ teaspoon freshly ground black pepper

Crush the garlic with the salt then pound in the parsley (or use a food processor but do not process to a smooth paste). Beat in the olive oil and lemon juice then add the remaining ingredients and stir well together.

CHERMOULA 2

A RECIPE FROM ESSAOUIRA

This recipe was given to me by a spice merchant – which may explain why it contains more spices than is usual. Instead of adding the lemon juice to the chermoula, *Youssef cooked the fish on a bed of slices of green lemon. It is rare for men to cook in Morocco, but he reassured me that this was his mother's recipe. Mix together all the ingredients and spread into the fish.*

1 teaspoon ground cumin

½ teaspoon of ground coriander

1 teaspoon paprika

¼ teaspoon cayenne pepper

Salt to taste

3 cloves garlic, peeled and finely chopped

4 tablespoons finely chopped fresh flat-leaf parsley

4 tablespoons of olive oil

CHERMOULA 3

A RECIPE FROM FEZ

Most of the recipes for cooking fish in Fez come from the Jewish quarter, where vinegar is preferred to lemon juice to compensate for the fattiness of river fish such as carp. But refrigerated lorries mean sea fish are now also available in Fez and I was given this recipe for sea bass. Mix together all the ingredients and spread into the fish.

2 cloves garlic

Sea salt

½ teaspoon ground cumin

1 teaspoon paprika

¼ teaspoon cayenne pepper

3 tablespoons finely chopped fresh coriander

1 tablespoon finely chopped fresh flat-leaf parsley

1 tablespoon finely chopped celery leaves

Juice of ½ a lemon

½ a preserved lemon, finely chopped

2 tablespoons olive oil

GRILLED SEA BASS WITH CHERMOULA

2 × 750g (1½lb) sea bass

Chermoula 3 (see page 57)

Make several deep slashes across the flesh on either side of the fish. Spread the *chermoula* all over the fish, making sure plenty gets down into the slashes. Leave to marinate for 2 to 3 hours.

Preheat the grill to maximum or better still get the barbecue coals glowing. Grill the fish close to the heat for 15 minutes on either side.

BAKED MULLET WITH CHERMOULA

2 × 750g (1½lb) mullet or sea bream

Chermoula 1 (see page 56)

For this recipe the *chermoula* should be almost a paste – this is most easily achieved by processing the garlic, parsley and spices with a little water.

Make several deep slashes on either side of the fish, right down to the bone. Spread the mixture all over the fish, making sure plenty gets down into the slashes. Marinate for 2 to 3 hours or better still overnight.

When you are ready to cook, preheat the oven to 180°C/350°F/gas mark 4. Loosely wrap each fish individually in foil and bake for 50 minutes, or until well-cooked through.

FISH TAGINE WITH CHERMOULA
TAGINE DE POISSON

Essaouira on Morocco's Atlantic coast has, despite its popularity with tourists, managed to retain much of its charm, largely because it still boasts an active fishing fleet. Sea bream would be the most typical fish for this tagine but you could also use sea bass, snapper and even cod. The lemons and carrots on the base of the tagine not only scent the fish but prevent it from sticking to the base of the tagine, which needs to be placed over direct heat. Traditionally it would be cooked over charcoal.

4 × 175g (6oz) fish steaks or
1 whole fish

Sea salt

Chermoula 2 (see page 57)

2 lemons

125g (4½oz) marinated green olives

3 large carrots, peeled

3 large tomatoes, peeled, deseeded and roughly chopped

Wash the fish well with salt and water. Rub the *chermoula* into the fish and leave for 30 minutes. Meanwhile, slice the lemons finely, rinse the olives and cut the carrots into batons. Arrange the lemon slices over the base of a tagine or other earthenware lidded dish which resists direct heat. Place the carrot batons in a lattice work over the lemons and lay the fish steaks on top. Cover with the olives and finally the tomatoes. Put on the lid and place over medium heat, 30 minutes for fish steaks or 45 minutes for a whole fish, until the fish is cooked through.

FISH KEBABS

This is a Tunisian recipe which should be served with the spicy sauce known as harissa *(see recipe page 155).*

750g (1½lb) filleted monkfish

¼ teaspoon saffron strands

2 tablespoons warm water

2 cloves garlic, peeled

½ teaspoon sea salt

½ teaspoon cayenne pepper

½ teaspoon ground cinnamon

4 tablespoons olive oil

Juice of 1 orange

3 tablespoons finely chopped fresh coriander

3 tablespoons finely chopped fresh flat-leaf parsley

Slice the fish across the grain into 2.5 cm (1 in) squares. Steep the saffron in the water for 10 minutes. Meanwhile crush the garlic with the salt to a paste. Add the spices then beat in the olive oil and the orange juice. Stir in the saffron water and finally add the chopped herbs.

Put the fish pieces into this mixture to marinade, turning them well to make sure they are thoroughly coated. Leave to marinate for at least 2 hours or preferably overnight.

When you are ready to cook preheat the grill to maximum. Thread four pieces of fish onto each kebab skewer and cook for a total of 6 to 7 minutes, turning several times and basting with the remains of the marinade. Serve with rice and *harissa*.

MONKFISH IN MOZARABIC STYLE
RAPE MOZARABE

Nowhere else in southern Spain do the Moors still haunt the streets as powerfully as in the great city of Córdoba, where the Mesquita looms among the narrow whitewashed houses. Although the Spanish clerics later filled in the sides of the mosque and even built a cathedral within its interior, they failed to disturb the essential harmony of the striped pillars and arches marching towards the exquisite mihrab. *After sitting in the cool courtyard, where the orange trees are aligned with the pillars within, cross the street to the stylish restaurant El Caballo Rojo, whose owners Pepe and José Manuel have dedicated themselves to researching and cooking ancient recipes in the mozarabic style – such as this one.*

750 g (1½ lb) monkfish tail

600 ml (1 pint) water

6 black peppercorns

1 large Spanish onion, peeled and finely sliced

3 tablespoons of olive oil

60 g (2 oz) sultanas

¼ teaspoon saffron strands

175 ml (6 fl oz) fruity white wine

60 g (2 oz) pine nuts

Sea salt

Cut the monkfish off the tail bone (reserve this for stock) and slice the flesh into large chunks about 5 cm (2 in) square. Pour the measured water into a pan, add the tail bone, and with the peppercorns simmer actively for 20 minutes to make a light stock. Strain the stock and pour over the sultanas. Leave to stand for 15 minutes then drain, reserving 175 ml (6 fl oz) of the liquid. Place the saffron to steep in this liquid.

In a large heavy pan, heat the olive oil over a medium heat and add the onion. Fry for 10 minutes, stirring frequently, until golden.

Turn the heat up to medium high and add the monkfish pieces to the pan. Fry for 3 to 4 minutes, turning several times, until slightly golden. Now add the wine to the pan and allow to bubble fiercely for 1 minute. Add the saffron liquid, the sultanas and pine nuts and a good pinch of salt. Bring to the boil then turn the heat to low and leave to simmer for 10 minutes. Check seasoning before serving.

SPICY PRAWNS

CREVETTES AUX ÉPICES

4 tablespoons olive oil

4 cloves garlic, peeled and finely chopped

1 teaspoon paprika

1 teaspoon ground cumin

½ teaspoon ground ginger

½ teaspoon freshly ground black pepper

¼ teaspoon cayenne

750 g (1½ lb) large uncooked prawns, peeled

4 tablespoons chopped fresh coriander

4 tablespoons chopped fresh flat-leaf parsley

Sea salt

Heat the oil and garlic together in a large heavy frying pan over a medium heat. When the garlic starts to sizzle add the spices and stir well. Now add the prawns and fry for 5 minutes, until the prawns are pink and cooked through. Add the herbs and salt to taste, fry for a further minute and serve very hot.

SMALL FRIED FISH

POISSONS EN FRITURE

350 g (12 oz) very small fish, such as whitebait

Sea salt and freshly ground black pepper

2 teaspoons paprika

½ teaspoon cayenne pepper

1 teaspoon ground cumin

250 g (9 oz) very fine couscous or semolina flour

Sunflower oil for frying

Chermoula 2, to serve (see page 57)

Wash the fish and dry well. Mix the seasoning and spices into the couscous. Heat the oil in a shallow pan and when it is nearly smoking roll a few of the fish at a time in the couscous and then put them immediately in the hot oil. Cook until they are nicely browned then drain on kitchen paper. Continue until all the fish are cooked, taking care never to overcrowd the pan. Serve with *chermoula 2*.

GRILLED SPICED SARDINES

MORUNA

In the Spanish village of Benalauría, which clings to a steep hillside in the Serranía mountain range above Malága, the fight of the Christians to expel the Moors is re-enacted each year. But on the menu of the village's only restaurant, the little Méson la Molienda, memories of the Moors linger all year round. I was delighted to be able to choose from cordero en salsa de almendras (young lamb in almond sauce), venao a la canela (venison cooked with cinnamon), sopa de almendras, a thin but full flavoured broth at the bottom of which lurked whole almonds, and moruna – Moorish style sardines. The meal finished with quinces preserved in sugar syrup and cinnamon. But with the coffee came distinctly unmoorish whole chestnuts liberally soaked in brandy.

12 fresh sardines

1 teaspoon sea salt

½ teaspoon ground cinnamon

2 teaspoons ground cumin

A pinch of nutmeg

1 teaspoon paprika

1 teaspoon freshly ground black pepper

6 tablespoons olive oil

2 tablespoons finely chopped fresh coriander

1 lemon

Wash the fish with the salt inside and out to slightly dry them out, and make several slashes on either side of the flesh. Mix the spices into the oil and smear this all over the fish. Leave to stand for 2 hours.

Either grill the fish over charcoal or under a very hot grill, for 5 minutes on either side. Baste regularly with the marinade during cooking. Sprinkle with the coriander and serve with quarters of lemon and plenty of bread.

TUJUBI'S TAGINE OF SARDINES

This recipe comes from a cookery book written in thirteenth century Andalucia by Tujubi.
Although some of the recipes were more complicated and richer than would be usual today, they
show the antecedents of Moroccan cooking as we know it. Tagine of sardines remains a popular
dish today but now it is usually made with tomatoes as in the next recipe for tagine of
anchovies. Tujubi's technique was the same but he used coriander, mint, fennel and onions for
the sauce. The complex flavours mingle perfectly, the sharpness of the herbs cutting through the
rich oiliness of the fish.

8 sardines

Sea salt

4 tablespoons of finely chopped
coriander

2 tablespoons of finely chopped
mint

½ a fennel bulb, including feathery
fronds, all finely chopped

1 onion, peeled and finely chopped

½ teaspoon of ground ginger

1 teaspoon of ground cinnamon

2 tablespoons of olive oil

Wash the sardines with salt and fillet them (see
tagine of anchovies page 67). Preheat the oven to
200°C/400°F/gas mark 6.

Mix together the herbs, chopped fennel bulb, onion
and spices. Spread a layer over the base of a small
round earthenware dish and add some sardine fillets
skin side up. Sprinkle over some of the herb mixture,
put another layer of fish fillets and continue until
you have no fish left, ending with a layer of herbs.
Pour over the oil and bake for 20 minutes, until the
surface is lightly browned.

TAGINE OF ANCHOVIES

TAGIN DE BOQUERONES

Driving south towards Fez from the pretty blue and white hilltop town of Chefchaouen, I came to a Sunday market on the border line of the old Spanish and French protectorates. Two local Berber women, wearing the distinctive red and white striped cloth and conical straw hats which are the traditional clothing of the women of the Rif, invited me to join them for lunch at one of the makeshift stalls. Although we were some distance from the sea, there was a busy trade in grilled anchovies and sardines, served straight from the charcoal with nothing but a sprinkling of salt and cumin. But even more popular were the little tagines of anchovies in a garlicky tomato sauce, which sat sizzling over the heat. There was general hilarity when I asked for the recipe – no one could believe that I wanted to recreate this peasant dish at home.

6 cloves garlic, peeled and finely chopped

4 tablespoons olive oil

1 kg (2 lb) tomatoes, peeled, deseeded and roughly chopped

1 teaspoon ground cumin

2 teaspoons paprika

¼ teaspoon cayenne

Sea salt to taste

4 tablespoons chopped fresh coriander

2 tablespoons chopped fresh flat-leaf parsley

20 fresh anchovies or 10 fresh sardines

First make the tomato sauce. Put a heavy pan over a medium heat and add the garlic and oil. When the garlic begins to sizzle, add the tomatoes, spices and salt. Mix the herbs together, reserve 2 tablespoons and add the rest to the pan. Leave to cook for 20 minutes, stirring occasionally.

Meanwhile fillet the anchovies or sardines by first cutting off the head. With a sharp knife split them down the belly, remove the innards and wash well. Press down on the anchovy or sardine with the flat of your hand on the backbone then turn it over and pull out the backbone. Remove any spare bones.

Preheat the oven to 220°C/425°F/gas mark 7. Choose a small round earthenware bowl and put a layer of tomato sauce in the base. Spread over half the anchovy or sardine fillets then add another layer of tomato sauce and half the remaining herbs. Cover with the remaining fillets, skin side up, then add the last of the sauce and the herbs. Bake in the oven for 15 minutes and serve with plenty of bread.

SARDINE BALLS

BOULETTES DE SARDINE

This is a Jewish recipe from Safi on the western Atlantic coast of Morocco. Safi once had a large Jewish community but as elsewhere in the country there are now only a few Jewish families left. Visiting Jewish tourists now seek out this speciality in private homes. The boulettes can be eaten straight away just as they are or bathed in a fresh tomato sauce.

8 sardines

Sea salt

2 cloves garlic, peeled and crushed

1 teaspoon ground cumin

1 teaspoon ground coriander

1 teaspoon paprika

¼ teaspoon cayenne

Flour

Olive oil for frying

FOR THE TOMATO SAUCE

3 tablespoons olive oil

500 g (1 lb) plum tomatoes, peeled, deseeded and roughly chopped

Salt

1 teaspoon white sugar

1 teaspoon paprika

½ teaspoon ground cumin

First make the tomato sauce. Heat the oil in a heavy pan and add the tomatoes, salt to taste, sugar and spices. Cook over a gentle heat for 20 minutes, until the tomatoes have broken down to form a thick sauce.

Fillet the sardines (see tagine of anchovies page 67) and soak the fillets in warm water for 5 minutes. After this time the skin should slip off easily – remove as much as possible. Sprinkle the skinned fillets with salt and leave to stand for 30 minutes; rinse well. Process the fillets with the garlic and spices to a smooth paste. Sprinkle with flour and with floured hands mould the paste into walnut sized balls. Fill a frying pan with olive oil to a depth of 1 cm (½ in) and when the oil is hot add the boulettes, frying them for 5 to 6 minutes and turning several times during the process.

Add the fried *boulettes* to the tomato sauce and cook for a further 5 minutes before serving.

OVEN-BAKED TUNA WITH SALSA

TONNO AL FORNO CON SALSA

The great tuna canneries may have closed, but on the island of Favignana, off Trapani at the very western end of Sicily, they still practise the ancient Arab art of the mattanza *to catch the tuna which migrate past their shores each June. I had heard the* rais *(captain) leading the old Arabic chants, his deep booming voice rising above the drum beat as the nets are hauled in by hand. When I meet Gioackino Kataldo he fulfilled all my expectations – a huge man with a gap-toothed smile and arms that looked thick enough to snap the wire cords used to haul in the catch.*

Tuna is often served with capers, as here in a sharp mint salsa. The best capers in Sicily (no mean claim) are reputed to come from Pantelleria, the furthest of the Trapani islands at a mere 70km from the Tunisian shore.

FOR THE FISH

4 tuna steaks, at least 2.5 cm (1 in) thick

3 tablespoons extra virgin olive oil

1 lemon, sliced

4 garlic cloves

1 sprig rosemary

1 sprig oregano

Coarse sea salt and freshly ground black pepper

4 tablespoons dry white wine

FOR THE SAUCE

1 tablespoon capers

2 tablespoons red wine vinegar

2 teaspoons sugar

Juice of ½ a lemon

4 tablespoons extra virgin olive oil

1 garlic clove, finely chopped

2 tablespoons finely chopped fresh mint

Arrange the tuna steaks in an earthenware oven dish in which they will just fit. Pour over the olive oil, arrange slices of lemon on top of the fish, tuck in the garlic and the herbs. Finally season well and leave to stand for 30 minutes.

Preheat the oven to 180°C/350°F/gas mark 4.

Assemble the salsa. Soak the capers in water for 10 minutes, drain and pat dry. Mix the vinegar and sugar together well then add the lemon juice. Slowly beat in the olive oil then add the garlic, chopped mint and capers.

Bake the tuna in the oven for 7 minutes then add the wine and bake for a further 5 minutes. Remove the fish from the aromatics and serve with the salsa.

SWORDFISH WITH PINE NUTS AND RAISINS

PEZ ESPADA EN CASSOLA

This recipe was found by Colman Andrews in Libre del Coch, *a Catalan cookbook published in Barcelona in 1520, although believed to have been written some thirty years earlier. With its fruits and nuts, its citrus sauce thickened with almonds and herbs, it is the sort of dish that would have appealed to the Moors, although they would have been more likely to cook meat rather than fish in this way. But the people of Barcelona have long been addicted to their seafood and it is no surprise that they adapted Moorish cooking habits to their favourite ingredient. Although the author of the* Libre del Coch *suggests this dish be made with swordfish (or* emperador, *emperor, as he called it) the recipe also works well with tuna.*

1 tablespoon whole blanched almonds

1 tablespoon finely chopped fresh flat-leaf parsley

1 sprig fresh mint

1 sprig marjoram

4 × 2.5 cm (1 in) thick swordfish or tuna steaks

Sea salt and freshly ground black pepper

Plain white flour

2 tablespoons olive oil

60 g (2 oz) raisins

150 ml (5 fl oz) dry white wine

Juice of 1 orange

Juice of ½ a lemon

60 g (2 oz) pine nuts

Pound together the whole almonds and the herbs to a knobbly consistency.

Season the fish well then dredge in flour. Heat the oil in large heavy pan and fry the fish for 2 minutes on either side, until lightly browned. Remove the fish with a slotted spoon and blot dry on kitchen paper. Soak the raisins in a little warm water.

Add the wine to the pan in which the fish cooked and bring rapidly to the boil, scraping the pan with a wooden spoon to amalgamate any crusty pieces. Add the orange and lemon juice to the wine and bubble fiercely for several minutes, until the sauce has reduced by about half to a thick syrupy consistency. Stir in the almond and herb *picada* (see rabbit with meat sauce page 107), followed by the drained raisins and the pine nuts. Turn the heat beneath the pan to low and add the fish to the sauce. Cook for 6 to 8 minutes, until the fish is cooked through, and serve.

SARDINES ESCABECHE

The Moors disapproved of wine (although in the tolerant society of al-Andaluz the vineyards flourished) but happily used wine vinegar as a preservative. Today escabèche is found not only all around the Western Mediterranean but as far afield as the Caribbean, where it is thought to have been introduced by Spanish and Portuguese sailors. Originally the escabèche technique was used only for meat, particularly game (see the recipe for partridge escabèche, page 104) but it soon became adapted to fish. The sharp sauce particularly suits oily fish like the sardine – this particular dish comes from Portugal, where sardines are practically the national dish.

8 sardines

Plain flour

150 ml (5 fl oz) olive oil

150 ml (5 fl oz) red wine vinegar

2 tablespoons white sugar

1 medium onion, peeled and thinly sliced into half moons

1 teaspoon whole black peppercorns

1 teaspoon whole coriander seeds

2 cloves

2 small dried red chillies

½ teaspoon coarse sea salt

2 fresh bay leaves

2 sprigs fresh rosemary

2 sprigs fresh fennel leaves

2 cloves garlic, peeled and crushed

2 pieces lemon zest

2 pieces orange zest

Gut and scale the sardines and rinse well under plenty of cold running water. Pat the fish dry and dust lightly with flour.

Heat two thirds of the oil in a heavy pan and fry the sardines in two batches for 3 minutes on either side, until lightly browned. Place the fried sardines side by side in an earthenware dish.

Add all the remaining ingredients except for the rest of the olive oil to the pan, bring to the boil and reduce to a slow simmer. Cook for 15 minutes, stirring frequently, then add the remaining olive oil and pour the contents of the pan over the fried fish. Leave to stand for at least 4 hours, turning the fish several times in the marinade. Serve cold with plenty of bread.

MARINATED MONKFISH

RAPE EN ADOBO

The town of Carmona, perched on a hillside above the plain east of Seville, was a favourite with both the Romans and the Moors. Sitting under the shade of a palm tree in the central square, I nibbled on a tapa of cazon en adobo *– baby shark in the spicy vinegar marinade the very name of which is derived from the Arabic. As* cazon *is a little hard to come by, I suggest you use the Spaniard's favourite fish, monkfish, instead.*

500 g (1 lb) monkfish

3 cloves garlic, peeled and crushed

1 teaspoon paprika

½ teaspoon ground cumin

½ teaspoon black pepper

¼ teaspoon cayenne pepper

1 teaspoon sea salt

250 ml (8 fl oz) white wine vinegar

50 ml (2 fl oz) water

Sunflower oil for deep-frying

Plain white flour

Cut the monkfish into 2.5 cm (1 in) pieces and place in an earthenware dish. Beat together the spices, salt, vinegar and water and pour over the fish. Leave to marinate for at least 4 hours.

When you are ready to eat, heat plenty of oil in a heavy pan. Lift the pieces of fish out of the marinade, pat dry and dredge in flour. When the oil is very hot fry the fish in several batches until golden and serve straight away.

SARDINES IN THE STYLE OF FIG-PICKERS'

SARDE A BECCAFICCO

The little Trattoria Stella lies on the edge of the crumbling Arab quarter of Palermo, the Kalsa. So unprepossessing from the outside that I walked straight past it, it is the haunt of local businessmen who know their food. Their version of the classic Sicilian dish of sarde a beccaficco *could have come straight from the court of the Caliphs. The dish gains its name from the little fig-picking birds which the rolled and stuffed sardines are said to resemble, and for the first time here I saw the point. The artfully stuffed fillets of fish glimmered silver, the tails of the sardines pointing upwards just like the fan of a bird's tail, each round plump body separated by the green of a bay leaf. Almost too beautiful to eat – but not quite. The stuffing of spiced breadcrumbs studded with nuts and what I latter discovered was candied orange peel was positively medieval in flavour. I prepare a slightly simpler version at home.*

8 small fresh sardines, cleaned, with heads removed but not the tails

2 cloves garlic

60 g (2 oz) sultanas

45 g (1½ oz) pine nuts

2 tablespoons chopped fresh flat-leaf parsley

60 g (2 oz) soft white breadcrumbs

Zest and juice of ½ an orange

½ teaspoon of ground cinnamon

¼ teaspoon of ground nutmeg

Freshly ground black pepper

10 fresh bay leaves

2 tablespoons olive oil

First prepare the sardines. With a sharp knife, split them along the belly from the head to almost the tail. Carefully prise them open and remove the backbone, taking care to pick out any stray bones. Lay each opened sardine down flat on its back.

Now prepare the stuffing. Chop the garlic, raisins and pine nuts very finely. Mix in the parsley, breadcrumbs, orange zest and juice, cinnamon, nutmeg and a little pepper. Preheat the oven to 200°C/400°F/gas mark 6.

Choose an earthenware dish. Spread a tablespoon of the stuffing over the flesh side of each sardine then roll the fish up into a round. Place joint side down in the dish with the tail sticking up. Repeat with the next sardine and place alongside with two bay leaves between. Repeat with the remaining sardines and bay leaves. Dribble over the olive oil. Bake for 12 to 15 minutes.

MEAT, POULTRY AND GAME

ABOVE: SPICES FOR SALE IN THE SOUK, MARRAKESH. *RIGHT:* AID EL KEBIR, *THE FEAST OF THE LAMB.*

The Moroccans are great meat eaters – or at least aspire to be. But meat has always been expensive and so the poorer rural communities developed a whole range of dishes in which small quantities of meat were cooked with vegetables for the dishes known as tagines, or for the famous couscous.

Mutton is by far the most widely used red meat, although beef is used for tagines and kefta – I prefer beef to mutton in the rich sweet tagines, although the very point of the classic *mrouzia* is the lamb. Kid is a special treat. No part of the animal is wasted, so offal plays an important role and skewered spicy lamb's liver grilled over charcoal is a Berber favourite. Pork is cooked with spices in Spain, as in the famous kebabs known as *pinchos morunos* or Moorish thorns, but of course remains taboo in Muslim Morocco and Tunisia. Chicken is probably the most popular meat of all, but birds such as quail, partridge and pigeon make frequent appearances.

Tagines gain their name from the earthenware cooking pot with its tapering conical lid in which they are cooked. The shape of the lid is important, as it keeps in the heat while the contents of the dish slowly simmer. Tagines can be made with meat, poultry, game, fish or just vegetables, they can be sweet, flavoured with dried fruits and nuts, or sharp, cut with lemon and fresh herbs, but the essence is in the slow cooking. Spices are added straight to the cooking liquid (typically water) or marinade rather than first tempered with heat. The result is tender ingredients in a gently spiced sauce with several layers of flavour. Traditionally tagines are cooked over charcoal, which lends a particular flavour to the dish, and take less well to the fiercer heat of gas or electricity. So if you are using an earthenware cooking pot of this kind, place a heat diffuser under it; otherwise use a heavy lidded casserole.

SWEET TAGINE OF LAMB WITH RAISINS AND ALMONDS

MROUZIA

Mrouzia *is a Berber speciality prepared for* Aid el Kebir *or the Feast of the Lamb. It originates from a time before refrigeration, when the ritual slaughter meant that there was far too much fresh lamb and means had to be found to conserve it. Hence this extraordinary dish, where the meat is preserved in butter and honey. The famous spice mix* ras el hanout *(see page 7) is traditionally used for* Mrouzia *but it can also be made with a much simpler mix of spices. This is a very sweet, very rich dish and should only be consumed in small quantities.*

1 kg (2 lb) neck of lamb, cut into pieces

3 teaspoons *ras el hanout* (or 1 teaspoon each ground pepper, ginger and cinnamon)

½ teaspoon saffron strands

1 stick cinnamon

125 g (4½ oz) unsalted butter

1 onion, peeled and grated

200 g (7 oz) whole blanched almonds

300 g (11 oz) seedless raisins

6 tablespoons dark honey

1 teaspoon ground cinnamon

Rub the *ras el hanout* or other spices into the meat. Steep the saffron in a litle warm water. Place the meat in a heavy casserole with the saffron water, cinnamon stick, butter, onion and almonds and enough water to just cover. Bring to the boil and simmer for 1½ hours, checking occasionally that there is sufficient water. When the meat is cooked add the raisins, honey and ground cinnamon. Cook slowly for a further 20 to 30 minutes, uncovered, until the honey has reduced to a syrupy glaze.

The *Mrouzia* will keep in the refrigerator for more than a week – in Morocco they keep it for over a month.

TAGINE OF LAMB WITH QUINCE

TAGINE D'AGNEAU AUX COINGS

*The quince was beloved by the Moors for its perfume and in medieval times to give a quince to
a lady was a declaration of love. In early autumn in Morocco the souks are full of baskets of
these knobbly fruit with their downy skin and those which are not used in tagines are preserved
in sugar syrup.*

750g (1½lb) lamb on the bone,
preferably leg, cut into large chunks

2 Spanish onions, peeled and
grated

60g (2½oz) butter

½ teaspoon ground ginger

1 teaspoon ground black pepper

½ teaspoon saffron strands

1 stick cinnamon

600ml (1 pint) water

Sea salt

2 large quince

2 teaspoons runny honey

½ teaspoon of ground cinnamon

Place the lamb, grated onion, butter, ginger, pepper,
saffron and stick of cinnamon in a heavy pan with a
lid. Place over a gentle heat and cook for 10 minutes,
stirring regularly, until the butter has melted and the
spices start to give off their aroma – the meat should
not brown. Add the water, bring to a simmer, cover
and leave to cook for 45 minutes, until the meat is
tender. At this stage, add salt to taste.

Cut each quince into 8 pieces and remove the core
but do not peel. Drop the quince into the pan and
stir in the honey and ground cinnamon (you may
need to add a little more water – the quince should
be just covered). Continue to simmer for 30
minutes, until the quince is tender.

LAMB AND APRICOT TAGINE
TAGINE D'AGNEAU AUX ABRICOTS

It is said that it was from the Persians that the Moors learnt the habit of cooking fruit with meat. It is in these fruit and meat dishes, which are still widely found in Morocco today, that we can see the clearest echoes of the tastes of medieval Britain. The spices used are ancient ones, ginger, cinnamon, nutmeg and pepper – the 'gold' of the spice route. Apricots grow abundantly on the terraced mountain slopes and are dried in the sun so that their sweet sharp flavour can be enjoyed all year round.

115g (4oz) dried apricots

550g (1¼lb) shoulder of lamb, off the bone, trimmed of fat and cut into chunks

1 teaspoon powdered ginger

1 teaspoon ground cinnamon

½ teaspoon freshly ground black pepper

A pinch of mace or nutmeg

1 large onion, peeled and grated

45g (1½oz) unsalted butter

1 small bunch fresh coriander

1 small bunch fresh flat-leaf parsley

Sea salt

Pour sufficient boiling water over the apricots to just cover them and leave to soak. Place the meat in a large heavy casserole or better still a tagine if you have one. Sprinkle over the spices, the grated onion and the butter cut into small pieces. Place the casserole over a low heat and cook for 5 minutes, stirring regularly, until the butter melts and the spices give off their scent – the meat should not brown. Tie the herbs together in a bunch and add them to the pot. Pour in just enough water to barely cover the meat. Bring to the boil then turn down the heat and leave to simmer gently for 1 hour.

Now add the apricots to the tagine, together with their liquid and salt to taste. Cook for a further 30 minutes, until the apricots are plumped up. Taste to check the seasoning, remove the bunches of herbs and serve with flat bread.

TAGINE OF BEEF WITH PRUNES

TAGINE DE VIANDE AUX PRUNES

The sweet tagines, particularly beloved by the people of Fez – home to ceremonial court cuisine – are some of the most extraordinary dishes of Moroccan cooking, at least to western tastes. They have their roots deep in a medieval tradition, where sweetness meant wealth, and have changed little over the centuries.

500g (1lb) braising beef

1 large onion, peeled and grated

½ teaspoon sea salt

½ teaspoon freshly ground black pepper

½ teaspoon saffron strands

½ teaspoon ground ginger

1 cinnamon stick

1 bunch fresh coriander

50g (2oz) butter

200g (7oz) prunes

1 tablespoon runny honey

1 tablespoon sesame seeds

Cut the beef into 4 pieces and place in a tagine or casserole. Add the grated onion, salt, spices, coriander and the butter. Pour over enough water to cover, place over a gentle heat, cover and leave to cook for 1½ hours, checking occasionally that there is sufficient water to prevent sticking, but remembering that the eventual sauce should be much reduced.

Remove the bunch of coriander, add the prunes to the dish and cook for a further 15 minutes. Stir in the honey and cook for another 15 minutes, until the prunes have plumped up and the meat has become very tender.

Meanwhile toast the sesame seeds in a dry frying pan until golden brown, taking care that they do not burn. Scatter these over the tagine before serving.

TAGINE OF BEEF WITH PUMPKIN

TAGINE DE VIANDE AU POTIRON

This recipe comes from Dar Loubana in Essaouira, an eighteenth century riad *which has been converted into a restaurant. Sitting in the courtyard open to the sky, with the pillared tiers of the house rising around us, we tucked into a succulent beef and pumpkin dish sweetened with honey. When I asked for the recipe the elderly female cook was too shy to come out and give it to me, and the owner was not keen for me to enter the kitchen, so in the face of my persistence an obliging waiter scuttled between my table and the chef until I understood how to prepare the dish. I just wish I could have met its cook.*

500g (1 lb) braising beef

1 large onion, peeled and grated

½ teaspoon sea salt

1 teaspoon ground cumin

1 teaspoon freshly ground black pepper

½ teaspoon ground ginger

1 teaspoon paprika

¼ teaspoon saffron strands

1 small bunch fresh flat-leaf parsley

1 small bunch fresh coriander

1 kg (2 lb) pumpkin

150 ml (5 fl oz) groundnut or sunflower oil

2 tablespoons runny honey

1 teaspoon ground cinnamon

Cut the beef into 4 pieces and place it in a tagine or heavy pot. Add the grated onion, salt, spices, the herbs tied in a bunch and sufficient water to just cover. Cover and place over a gentle heat. Leave to simmer for 2 hours.

Meanwhile peel the pumpkin and roughly chop the flesh. Place it in a heavy pan with the oil and cook over a moderate heat for 30 to 40 minutes, until the pumpkin is very tender and almost dissolving. Drain off the excess oil. Preheat the oven to 150°C/300°F/gas mark 2.

Mix the honey and cinnamon into the cooked pumpkin and place over a gentle heat. Cook for 10 minutes, mashing the pumpkin with a fork so that it becomes almost a purée.

When the beef is meltingly tender and the sauce has reduced to become thick and unctuous (if necessary remove the beef and briefly simmer the sauce down), remove the bunch of herbs and place the beef and its sauce in an earthenware serving dish. Spread the pumpkin mixture over the beef, place in the oven for 10 minutes to heat through and serve.

TAGINE OF LAMB WITH ARTICHOKES

TAGINE D'AGNEAU AUX ARTICHAUTS

This a tagine to serve in spring, when the small spiky purple artichokes which grow wild in Morocco are in season. Freshly podded peas are sometimes added to the tagine in the last 15 minutes of cooking, in which case the tomatoes should be left out. Serves 6 to 8.

1 kg (2 lb) lamb, cut into pieces

2 onions, peeled and grated

3 cloves garlic, peeled and finely chopped

¾ teaspoon freshly ground black pepper

¾ teaspoon ground ginger

¼ teaspoon saffron strands

½ teaspoon sea salt

2 tablespoons olive oil

4 artichokes

1 lemon

3 large tomatoes, peeled, seeded and chopped

3 tablespoons finely chopped fresh flat-leaf parsley

Place the lamb in a heavy pot or tagine and add the grated onion, garlic, spices, salt and oil. Pour in enough water to just cover the meat and place the pot over a moderate flame. Cook gently for about 1 hour, stirring occasionally, until the meat is tender.

Meanwhile remove the hearts from the artichokes (see page 41) and cut them into quarters. Place them in a large bowl of water with slices of lemon, to prevent them discolouring.

When the meat is tender, remove it from the sauce. Turn the heat up slightly, so that the sauce bubbles actively, and add the drained artichoke hearts.

When the artichokes have cooked for 15 minutes, add the chopped tomatoes and the parsley to the sauce. Continue to cook for a further 10 to 15 minutes, until the artichoke hearts are tender and the sauce thick. Return the meat to the pan to heat through, check the seasoning and serve.

BERBER LENTIL AND VEGETABLE TAGINE

TAGINE BERBÈRE

The Berbers, the original mountain people of Morocco who retain a distinct identity, are cultivators and goat and sheep herders who still live by the land. Their dishes reflect their living habits, being simple with a small amount of meat for added flavour – in fact their diet is probably a nutrionist's dream, for they eat a lot of bread, milk, grain (both semolina and barley), pulses and plenty of vegetables, the latter depending upon the season. Unlike most Moroccan tagines, this recipe has a distinct lack of spices; those are reserved for the wealthy of the city.

I got the recipe for this tagine from a roadside stall-holder in the beautiful Ourika valley south of Marrakesh, who was doing a roaring trade with day-trippers from the town who had travelled up the valley to see the famous seven waterfalls. On the way back, his simple tagines simmering over charcoal tempted them to stop. As one confirmed townie told me, 'there is nothing like fresh food in the mountains'. The stall-holder, despite his busy trade, was less delighted – 'these young people do not appreciate the taste of smen', *he told me – 'now I must use ordinary butter'. I must say I too have failed to acquire a taste for the rancid butter known as* smen *which the Berbers adore. But even without it this is a simple nourishing dish with plenty of flavour.*

300g (11oz) green lentils

250g (9oz) lamb on the bone (knuckle will do but shoulder is best)

60g (2½oz) butter

1 large onion, peeled and grated

1 bunch fresh coriander

2 tomatoes, peeled, deseeded and chopped

4 large carrots, peeled

350g (12oz) pumpkin or other squash, peeled

2 large red-skinned potatoes, peeled

Sea salt and freshly ground black pepper

Bring a large pot of water to the boil, add the lentils, boil hard for 5 minutes then drain. Put the lentils, lamb, three-quarters of the butter, the onion, coriander and tomatoes in a tagine or heavy cooking pot over a moderate heat, cover with water to a depth of 2.5cm (1in), and leave to simmer for 30 minutes.

Meanwhile cut the carrots, pumpkin and potato into thumb sized sticks. Add to the cooking pot, with more water to cover if necessary, together with plenty of salt and pepper. Cover and cook for another 45 minutes until the vegetables are very tender. Remove the bunch of coriander and stir in the remaining butter before serving.

TAGINE OF CHICKEN WITH EGGS

TAGINE S'AOURI

This is a truly medieval dish, a layer of chicken poached with herbs and saffron to give a scented but slightly bland meat, topped with slivers of preserved lemon, the meat hidden away under a topping of risen eggs. The recipe was given to me by a woman who must remain nameless but who was in an unhappy situation in her family home. This dish is like our family, she told me – lots of froth on top, slightly sour underneath.

2 chicken breasts

2 boneless chicken thighs

½ a large onion, peeled and grated

2 cloves garlic, peeled and finely chopped

4 tablespoons finely chopped fresh flat-leaf parsley

4 tablespoons finely chopped fresh coriander

2 tablespoons olive oil

½ teaspoon saffron strands

½ teaspoon freshly ground black pepper

Fine sea salt

1 preserved lemon, rinsed and cut into strips

5 medium eggs

Place the chicken in a tagine or heavy casserole with the onion, garlic, herbs, oil, saffron, pepper and salt to taste. Add just enough water to cover and cook over a gentle flame for 40 minutes, until the chicken is cooked through.

Preheat the oven to 180°C/350°F/gas mark 4.

Remove the chicken and cut into bite-sized pieces. Boil the sauce to reduce until it is very thick. Arrange the chicken pieces in a tagine and lay the strips of lemon over them. Ladle over the sauce. Cover and place in the oven for 10 minutes.

Meanwhile preheat the grill to three-quarters strength. Separate the eggs and beat the yolks. Whip the whites with a pinch of salt until they stand in peaks.

Fold the whipped whites into the beaten eggs and spread this mixture all over the chicken in the tagine. Place immediately under the preheated grill and cook for 6 to 7 minutes, until the top is browned and lightly risen. Serve straightaway.

CHICKEN BREASTS WITH PINE NUTS

PECHUGAS DE POLLO CON PINONES

The Moor's favourite nut was the almond, but they also liked to use the little kernels from the stone pines which ring the Mediterranean shores. Typically pine nuts were combined with savoury ingredients, as they still are throughout Spain. Here chicken breasts are cooked in a gently spiced sherry sauce, thickened in the traditional manner with bread rather than flour, and flecked with crunchy pine nuts.

4 boneless chicken breasts

3 tablespoons olive oil

1 Spanish onion, finely chopped

3 fat cloves garlic, crushed and finely chopped

1 thick slice dry white country bread, crusts removed

½ teaspoon ground cinnamon

1 clove, crushed

3 or 4 saffron strands

½ teaspoon crushed black peppercorns

50g (2oz) pine nuts

2 tablespoons chopped fresh flat-leaf parsley

100ml (3½floz) fino sherry, or very dry white wine

100ml (3½floz) water

Sea salt

Heat the oil in a heavy, large frying pan with a lid over a high heat. When the oil is really hot, fry the chicken breasts for 1 minute on either side, so that they are lightly browned. Remove the breasts from the oil and set aside, covered.

Turn the heat under the pan to medium low and add the chopped onion and garlic. Fry gently for 15 minutes, stirring regularly, until the onion is soft and golden. Turn the heat back to high and add the bread to the pan. Fry for 1 minute, until the bread soaks up the oil and turns golden, then add the spices and pine nuts to the pan. Fry for a further minute, stirring all the time, then add the sherry or wine and all but a teaspoon of the parsley. As soon as the sherry starts to bubble, add the water and finally a good pinch of salt.

Bring the sauce to the boil then turn down to a simmer, cover and leave to cook for 5 minutes. Return the chicken to the pan, spooning the sauce over the meat, cover and leave to cook over a medium low heat for 7 minutes. Turn the chicken over, cover and leave to cook for a further 6 to 7 minutes, until the chicken is cooked through. Taste the sauce to check seasoning, sprinkle with the remaining parsley and serve.

TAGINE OF CHICKEN WITH PRESERVED LEMON
TAGINE DE POULET M'QUALLI

Wherever they invaded, the Moors took with them their beloved citrus fruit trees, planting them in their courtyards so that they could enjoy the cool shade they produced, the fragrance of their blossom and finally the sharp scent of the ripe fruit. Moroccans today retain their love of the lemon in particular and conserve the fruit in salt so that it can be enjoyed all year round (see recipe page 152). These preserved lemons have a unique, almost honeyed flavour, shown at its best in this classic tagine of chicken with the cracked green olives for which Morocco (and Marrakesh in particular) is also famous.

1.35-1.5 kg (2½-3½ lb) chicken

3 cloves garlic, peeled and crushed

1 teaspoon coarse sea salt

1 small bunch fresh coriander, very finely chopped

Juice of ½ a lemon

1 large white onion, peeled and grated

1 teaspoon freshly ground black pepper

1 teaspoon ground ginger

¼ teaspoon saffron filaments

4 tablespoons olive oil

1 stick cinnamon

2 preserved lemons

175 g (6 oz) green cracked olives

Rub the garlic, salt, lemon juice and the coriander into the cavity of the chicken. Mix together the onion, spices and olive oil and rub over the outside of the chicken. Leave to stand for 30 minutes.

Place the chicken breast-side down in a tagine or heavy oval casserole, making sure you add all the marinade juices. Pour in sufficient water to cover two thirds of the chicken and add the stick of cinnamon. Bring the water to the boil, then reduce to a simmer and cook for 1 hour, turning the chicken several times during cooking. Preheat the oven to 150°C/300°F/gas mark 2.

Rinse the preserved lemons and olives under cold running water. Cut the preserved lemons into strips. Remove the chicken from the casserole if that is what you are using, place in an earthenware serving dish and cover with foil to keep warm (if you have a tagine, drain the sauce into a pan). Turn up the heat under the casserole for 5 minutes to reduce the sauce. Pour the sauce over the chicken in the tagine and add the olives and preserved lemons. Place in the oven for 10 minutes then serve.

CHICKEN WITH AUBERGINES

ALMORONIA

This is a recipe from the Jewish tradition, brought back to Morocco by the large Jewish communities who were expelled from al-Andaluz. It is typically served after the fast of Yom Kippur, when custom demands that one chicken should be slaughtered for each member of the family. I ate this dish in Tangier, where it is called almoronia *or the Moor but elsewhere in Morocco it is also found under the name of* el berania *or the stranger.*

1.25 kg (2¾ lb) chicken

1 litre (1¾ pints) water

1 teaspoon crushed black pepper

1 stick cinnamon

¼ teaspoon saffron strands

A pinch of sea salt

750 g (1¾ lb) aubergines

Sunflower or groundnut oil

2 large mild onions, peeled and sliced into half moons

3 tablespoons olive oil

1 clove garlic, peeled and finely chopped

1 tablespoon clear honey

Place the chicken in a large pot with the water and half the pepper, all the cinnamon, saffron and salt. Bring to the boil, turn down to a simmer and leave to cook for 50 to 60 minutes, turning the chicken several times during the cooking.

Meanwhile peel the aubergines in strips, so that you have one strip of skin followed by a strip of exposed flesh. Fill a frying pan with 1 cm (½ in) oil and when very hot fry the aubergines in several batches, browning them on both sides. Drain the aubergines on kitchen paper to remove excess oil.

Heat the olive oil in a heavy pan over a moderate heat and add the onions. Cook for 30 minutes, stirring regularly, until the onions are very tender. Preheat the oven to 150°C/300°F/gas mark 2. Stir the honey into the onions and add 2 ladles of the poaching stock from the chicken together with the remaining pepper. Cook for a further 10 minutes over a gentle heat.

The *almoronia* is now ready to be assembled. Place the aubergines in the bottom of an earthenware ovenproof dish. Joint the chicken and place over the aubergine slices. Finally pour over the onion sauce. Place in the oven and cook for 30 minutes.

CHICKEN M'HAMMAR

POULET M'HAMMAR

Whole small chickens are first poached in the usual manner with garlic, spices and herbs and then finished in butter to give them a crispy brown exterior, before being served with the poaching sauce. Some Moroccan cooks include the chicken livers and gizzards in the sauce but I find this too rich.

2 x 900g (2lb) chickens

Sea salt

2 onions, peeled and grated

4 cloves garlic, peeled and finely chopped

1 teaspoon paprika

½ teaspoon black pepper

¼ teaspoon saffron

½ teaspoon ground ginger

1 small bunch fresh coriander

1 small bunch fresh parsley

400ml (14floz) water

90g (3½oz) butter

1 tablespoon groundnut or sunflower oil

Choose a large heavy pot into which the chickens will just fit and place them in breast side down. Add the onion, garlic, spices, the herbs tied into a bunch and a pinch of salt. Pour in the water and bring to the boil. Turn down to a simmer, cover and leave to cook for 1¼ hours, turning the chickens several times.

When the chickens are cooked, remove them from the sauce. Melt the butter with the oil in a heavy pan or skillet and when the oil is hot add the chickens. Fry them over a medium heat for 20 minutes, turning regularly, until the skin is brown and crispy. Meanwhile remove the bunch of herbs from the sauce and reduce the sauce by half by fast boiling.

Serve the browned crispy chickens in a tagine or earthenware dish, with the sauce spooned around.

STEAMED BUTTERED SAFFRON CHICKEN

POULET À LA VAPEUR

Serves 2 to 3.

1.25 kg (2½ lb) chicken
Sea salt
1 teaspoon saffron strands
90 g (3½ oz) unsalted butter
½ a lemon
Whole cumin seeds

In order to draw the blood out before steaming, rub plenty of salt into the chicken, inside and out, and leave to stand for 10 minutes before washing well.

In a pestle and mortar, pound together half the saffron with half the butter. With your fingers carefully ease the chicken skin away from the flesh and smear the butter and saffron mixture between the two.

Fill the base of the steamer or couscoussier with water and add the lemon half. Place the steamer over a medium heat and bring the water to the boil. Put the chicken in the top half, cover and leave to cook for 25 to 30 minutes.

Meanwhile preheat the oven to 220°C/425°F/gas mark 7.

Pound together the remaining saffron, butter, a good pinch of salt and 1 teaspoon of cumin seeds. When the chicken is cooked and the legs fall easily away from the breast, remove it from the steamer and spread the butter mixture all over the surface of the bird. Place in the oven for 5 minutes and serve very hot, with little bowls of salt and cumin seeds.

CHICKEN BREASTS IN ORANGE SAUCE

PECHUGAS DE POLLO EN SALSA DE NARANJAS

This recipe comes from Valencia, queen of the oranges. It uses both the bitter orange which the Moors first planted and the sweet oranges which were introduced later. If you can't get Seville oranges the sauce is still good with just ordinary oranges, but add a squeeze of lemon as well. The final addition of chopped mint is a very Arab touch.

4 boneless chicken breasts, skin removed

Sea salt and freshly ground black pepper

50g (2oz) butter

1 tablespoon olive oil

Juice of 1 Seville orange

Juice of 2 sweet oranges

1 tablespoon finely chopped fresh mint

Season the chicken well. Choose a heavy frying pan with a lid in which all the breasts will fit, place it over a medium heat and add almost all the butter, reserving a knob, and the oil. When the butter is fizzing add the chicken and fry for 2 minutes on either side, until just coloured. Add the juice of the 3 oranges, cover and leave to simmer for 8 to 10 minutes, until the breasts are cooked through (cut into them to check).

Remove the chicken to keep warm and add the mint to the pan together with the remaining knob of butter. Allow to bubble for a minute then pour over the chicken and serve.

POT-ROASTED CHICKEN STUFFED WITH COUSCOUS

POULET FARCIE

Serves 4 to 6.

2 x 900 g (2 lb) chickens

Sea salt

200 g (7 oz) couscous

125 g (4½ oz) raisins

90 g (3½ oz) flaked almonds

60 g (2½ oz) butter

1½ teaspoons black pepper,
coarsely ground

½ teaspoon saffron strands

½ teaspoon ground cinnamon

6 teaspoons honey

1 onion, peeled and grated

1 stick cinnamon

½ teaspoon ground ginger

400 ml (14 fl oz) water

Rub plenty of salt into the chickens inside and out; pour sufficient boiling water over the couscous to cover by 1 cm (½ in). Pour sufficient warm water over the raisins to just cover. Leave all three to stand for 10 minutes. Fry the flaked almonds in half the butter, until they are just golden.

Wash the chickens well. Drain the raisins. Mix the raisins into the couscous, which will have absorbed all the water. Add the flaked almonds, ½ teaspoon of the pepper, ¼ teaspoon of the saffron, the ground cinnamon, salt to taste and 4 teaspoons of the honey.

Stuff the couscous mixture into the chickens, taking care not to fill too full as the couscous will swell during cooking. Sew up the aperture with a needle and thread. Reserve the remaining stuffing mixture to serve with the chickens.

Choose a heavy pot into which both chickens will just fit. Melt the remaining butter and add the the rest of the pepper, saffron, grated onion, cinnamon stick and ground ginger. Place the chickens breast down in the pot and add the water and a pinch of salt. Bring to the boil, turn down to a simmer, cover and leave to cook for 1¼ hours, turning the chickens several times during cooking.

When the chickens are cooked, remove and place in a tagine or earthenware serving dish. Turn the heat up under the sauce and reduce to half by fast boiling. Stir in the remaining honey, allow to boil for a further minute, pour over the chickens and serve with the rest of the couscous mixture.

SPANISH POT-ROAST LAMB

CALDERETA DE CORDERO

In a country short of water, pot-roasting is a sensible way of cooking. Even more so where few houses boast an oven, so that any oven-cooked dish requires a trip to the bakers. By the thirteenth century the tagine was a well-known way of cooking in southern Spain, and when the Arab invaders were expelled the habit of cooking a joint of meat with spices and oil in an earthenware covered pot over charcoal remained. There have been times in southern Spain where wine has been cheaper than water – so it makes sense to use it as a mixture here.

Half a shoulder of lamb on the bone, about 1.25 kg (2½ lb)

1 teaspoon coarse sea salt

1 teaspoon freshly ground black pepper

3 cloves

A good pinch of mace

1 teaspoon ground cinnamon

Zest and juice of ½ a lemon

3 tablespoons olive oil

1 large glass dry white wine

2 bay leaves

A sprig of fresh rosemary

Preheat the oven to 180°C/350°F/gas mark 4.

Mix together the salt, spices and lemon juice and rub all over the meat. Leave to stand for 30 minutes.

Choose an earthenware casserole into which the meat will just fit and tuck the meat in. Pour over the oil and wine and tuck in the herbs. Cook uncovered in the oven for 1½ hours, turning and basting the meat several times during the cooking process. Serve with saffron rice cooked in stock with a pinch of saffron.

CHICKEN STUFFED WITH RICE AND CHERMOULA
POULET FARCIE AU RIZ

This recipe is a favourite of my friend Oumkeltoun Abadi in Fez. Her family live in a magnificent house on the edge of the medina, recently turned into a palace restaurant called La Maison Bleue. Each evening Oumelktoun and her mother prepare a feast for their guests served in a family style – I enjoyed seven different salads, two tagines and a milk and almond pastilla.

Not surprisingly after all her work in the kitchen, when cooking for herself Oumelktoun prefers to turn to simpler recipes, such as this steamed chicken stuffed with rice flavoured with herbs and spices. Serves 2 to 3.

175g (6oz) long grain white rice

1 large bunch fresh coriander

1 large bunch fresh flat-leaf parsley

1 tablespoon finely chopped celery leaves

1 teaspoon paprika

1 teaspoon ground cumin

¼ teaspoon cayenne pepper

½ teaspoon sea salt

Juice of 1 lemon

1 preserved lemon, diced

½ a lemon

1.25kg (2½lb) chicken

Rinse the rice very thoroughly under cold running water to remove the starch – the water should run clear. Finely chop 4 tablespoons of coriander leaves and 2 tablespoons of parsley and mix this into the rice together with the celery leaves. Add the spices, salt, lemon juice and preserved lemon and loosely stuff the cavity of the chicken with this mixture.

Fill the base of the steamer or couscoussier with water and add the lemon half. Place the steamer over a medium heat and bring the water to the boil. Lay the bunches of herbs in the top half of the steamer or couscoussier and place the chicken on top. Cover and leave to steam for 40 minutes until the chicken is thoroughly cooked through and the rice plump. To check that the chicken is cooked pierce the flesh between the leg and breast – the juices should run clear.

STEAMED LAMB

AGNEAU À LA VAPEUR

Steaming meats is an ancient cooking method which really concentrates the flavour. In Morocco lamb is sometimes steamed with no added flavourings at all but I prefer to rub garlic and spices into the meat and lay it on a bed of herbs. As the meat steams the kitchen fills with aromatic scent.

Half a shoulder of lamb on the bone, about 1.25kg (2½lbs)

2 cloves garlic, peeled

1 teaspoon sea salt

1 teaspoon freshly ground black pepper

¼ teaspoon saffron strands

1 teaspoon paprika

¼ teaspoon cayenne pepper

3-4 tablespoons olive oil

½ a lemon

1 large bunch fresh coriander

Toasted cumin seeds to serve

Wash and dry the lamb well. Crush the garlic with the salt then add the pepper, saffron, paprika and cayenne pepper and crush again. Add just enough oil to make a smooth paste and smear this all over the lamb.

Three-quarters fill the base of the steamer with water, add the lemon half and bring to the boil. Turn down to a simmer and place the bunch of coriander in the base of the top half of the steamer. Lay the lamb on top, cover with a clean teatowel, firmly put on the lid and leave over a gentle heat for 1½ hours. Do not lift the steamer lid during cooking.

Serve with side bowls of toasted cumin seeds and sea salt, plenty of bread and a green salad.

GRILLED SPICED SPRING CHICKEN

If there is one dish that it is worth heating the barbecue coals for, this is it. The Moroccans tend to barbecue their chickens whole but elsewhere in the Mediterranean, particularly in Spain, they split them open to ensure maximum exposure of the flesh to the heat, so that you end up with the maximum ratio of charred flesh to juicy meat. The chickens should be served with little bowls of coarse sea salt, toasted cumin seeds, cayenne and paprika and quarters of lemon – plus plenty of flat bread to mop up the juices. Serves 2.

2 small spring chickens or poussins, spatchcocked

4 tablespoons olive oil

Juice of 1 lemon

1 teaspoon paprika

¾ teaspoon coarse sea salt

1 teaspoon ground cumin

¼ teaspoon cayenne pepper

2 tablespoons finely chopped fresh flat leaf parsley

Toasted cumin seeds

Mix together all the marinade ingredients and pour over the chickens. Leave for at least 2 hours.

Meanwhile, get the barbecue coals glowing and heat a ridged grill pan, or heat the grill to maximum. Grill the chickens for 25 to 30 minutes, placing them skin side down on the barbecue or grill pan and skin side up under the grill. Turn the chickens to expose the underside to the heat after 10 minutes and turn back after another 10 minutes so that you finish skin side to the heat source. Baste regularly with the marinade. Serve with quartered lemons and bowls of coarse sea salt and toasted cumin seeds.

ROASTED LAMB
M'CHOUI

The real m'choui is of course a whole lamb roasted in a pit over charcoal for feast days. Its flavour is incomparable but its preparation deeply impractical. You can get some of the taste of m'choui simply by marinating a whole leg of lamb with butter and spices and then roasting it in the oven, though calling it m'choui is perhaps unfair. However, this is still a very good dish, as long as you appreciate that the meat must be cooked until it falls off the bone rather than simply to fashionable pinkness. Serves 6 to 8.

2- 2.5 kg (4½-5½ lb) whole leg of lamb

1 teaspoon coarse sea salt

4 cloves garlic

2 teaspoons ground coriander

2 teaspoons ground cumin

1 teaspoon freshly ground black pepper

2 teaspoons paprika

½ teaspoon cayenne

175 g (6 oz) unsalted butter

TO SERVE

4 lemons, quartered

Whole toasted cumin seeds

Paprika

Coarse sea salt

With a sharp knife, make deep incisions all over the leg of lamb. Crush the garlic cloves with the salt to a paste. Add the spices and then pound in the butter. Smear this spice, garlic and butter mixture all over the lamb and leave to rest in a cool place for 4 hours at least.

When you are ready to cook, preheat the oven to 220°C/425°F/gas mark 7. Place the lamb fat-side up on a baking tray in the oven and cook for 20 minutes. Turn and baste with the spicy butter, cook for another 10 minutes. Turn again and lower the heat to 180°C/350°F/gas mark 4. Cook for a further 2 to 2½ hours, basting at least three times an hour, until a crisp crust has formed, while underneath the meat is very tender and falls off the bone.

Serve very hot with little bowls of lemon, cumin seeds, paprika and salt and plenty of bread. Theoretically your guests should tear off pieces with their fingers but you will probably find it easier to carve the leg.

KEBABS AND KEFTA

Kebabs are the food of the streets of Morocco, and nowhere more so than in Marrakesh's Djmaa el Fna, where each evening the kebab sellers set up their stalls. As the setting sun casts its brilliant red light across the square, its rays pierce through clouds of smoke hanging over the snake charmers, musicians and transvestite dancers. The men crowd in circles to watch the performance but every so often the scent of spice and sizzling fat will become irresistible and one or two will peel off from the ring to take their seats at the eating benches.

MINCED LAMB KEBABS
KEFTA

The key to good kebabs is that the lamb must be very finely minced with the other ingredients, until the mixture is smooth and paste-like. Moroccan cooks often still use a pestle and mortar or at least a hand-mincer to achieve this texture, a process aided by the fact that they like to include plenty of fat for flavour. I have found that a food processor works perfectly well. Serve with lemon, cumin seeds, salt and bread.

500g (1lb) finely minced lamb

1 large onion, peeled and finely grated

2 teaspoons ground cumin

3 teaspoons paprika

¼ teaspoon cayenne

1 teaspoon coarse sea salt

1 large bunch flat-leaf parsley, finely chopped

1 small bunch coriander, finely chopped

12 leaves fresh mint, finely chopped

Mix the lamb with the other ingredients. Either pound in a pestle and mortar for 10 minutes to achieve a smooth consistency or give a quick whizz in the food processor. Leave to stand for 1 hour for the flavours to mingle.

When you are ready to cook, wet your hands with a little water and take a piece of the meat mixture the size of a walnut. With your fingers mould this along the length of a metal skewer. The kebabs are best cooked over charcoal but can also be cooked under a preheated hot grill, or on a ridged grill pan placed over high heat. The kebabs should be turned frequently and thoroughly cooked through.

MOORISH STYLE KEBABS

PINCHOS MORUNOS

Arriving one evening in Baeza, a gem of a town set amidst the vast rolling olive fields of Jaén province in Southern Spain, I was astonished to find that in each little square in the perfect Renaissance centre a bar and a charcoal brazier had been set up in the open air. I had happened on one of the many fiestas in the month of May and the town was ready to party. First there was serious eating and drinking to be done. These spicy kebabs were by the far most popular tapas, washed down with the local white wine mixed with lemonade and sold in plastic bottles with a pouring spout fitted. As the night wore on, impromptu flamenco dancing broke out amongst the young while the old women stood in circles rhythmically clapping. Then one stepped forward to sing, a deep throaty lament that told of the sadness of centuries gone by. As each woman in turn took up the lament, encouraging the young to learn the words, I sat back and admired the very great sense of history which fills the Andalusian character.

625 g (1¼ lb) pork escalope, preferably with a little fat

1 teaspoon ground cumin

3 teaspoons paprika

½ teaspoon cayenne pepper

½ teaspoon turmeric

6 tablespoons olive oil

2 lemons, quartered

Sea salt

Cut the pork into 2 cm (¾ in) cubes. Mix together the remaining ingredients and pour over the cubes of pork, stirring well to make sure all are coated with the spicy oil. Leave to marinate for at least 4 hours, preferably overnight.

Thread 3 cubes of meat onto each kebab stick. Cook over charcoal or under a medium grill for 8 to 10 minutes, turning and basting frequently with the marinade. Serve with quarters of lemon and a bowl of sea salt.

TAGINE OF KEFTA IN SPICY LEMON SAUCE

TAGINE DE KEFTA AU CITRON

FOR THE KEFTA

500g (1lb) finely minced lamb

½ teaspoon sea salt

½ teaspoon freshly ground black pepper

¼ teaspoon cayenne pepper

¼ teaspoon of ground cinnamon

1 teaspoon ground cumin

1 tablespoon paprika

1 tablespoon chopped fresh flat-leaf parsley

2 large onions, peeled and grated

FOR THE SAUCE

3 tablespoons chopped fresh coriander

3 tablespoons chopped fresh flat-leaf parsley

1 teaspoon ground ginger

½ teaspoon freshly ground black pepper

½ teaspoon cumin

¼ teaspoon saffron strands

1 teaspoon paprika

2 small dried red chillies (optional)

45g (1½oz) butter

350ml (12floz) water

2 Spanish onions, grated

4 slices unwaxed lemon

Juice of 1 lemon

First make the kefta. Put the minced lamb into a bowl and mix in the spices and the parsley. Add one heaped tablespoon of the grated onion to the meat mixture and reserve the remainder for the sauce. Either pound the meat mixture or give a quick whizz in the processor – the mixture should be very smooth. With your hands form the mixture into balls about the size of walnuts.

Next, make the sauce. Take a large heavy frying pan with a lid and place the remaining grated onion, the spices, herbs, butter and water for the sauce in the pan and bring to the boil. Turn down to a gentle simmer, cover and leave to cook for 20 minutes.

Add the kefta to the sauce, together with the lemon slices. Cook for 30 minutes, turning the kefta frequently. Check the seasoning of the sauce, add the lemon juice and serve.

KEBAB WITH EGGS

KEBAB M'GHDOUR

Look in any medieval European cookbook and you will find eggs cooked with meat dishes to provide added richness. The cookbooks were commissioned by the wealthy and can be seen as a reflection of courtly rather than everyday cuisine, but this addition of eggs to meat dishes is one that has persisted in Morocco.

750g (1½lb) leg of lamb, cut into 2.5cm (1in) cubes

2 onions, peeled and grated

3 cloves garlic, peeled and finely chopped

Sea salt and freshly ground black pepper

60g (2½oz) butter

2 teaspoons paprika

1 teaspoon ground cumin

½ teaspoon cayenne pepper

2 tablespoons chopped fresh flat-leaf parsley

2 tablespoons chopped fresh coriander

1 stick cinnamon

350ml (12floz) water

Juice of 1 lemon

4 large eggs

Marinate the cubes of lamb with the grated onion, garlic, salt and pepper for at least 2 hours.

Cook the meat either on a heavy ridged grill pan directly over heat or under a very hot grill. Grill the meat for 2 minutes on either side, until nicely browned but not cooked through.

Melt the butter in a heavy pan over a gentle heat. Add the browned meat, the ground spices, the remains of the marinade and the chopped herbs. Cook over a gentle heat for 5 minutes, turning the meat regularly, until the scent of the spices rises. Tuck in the stick of cinnamon, pour over the water and bring to the boil. Turn the heat to low, so that the liquid just simmers, cover and leave to cook for 1 to 1¼ hours, until the meat is very tender. Preheat the oven to 180°C/350°F/gas mark 4.

When the meat is tender, lift it out of the sauce and arrange in a tagine or other ovenproof earthenware dish with a lid. Pour the lemon juice over the meat. Reduce the sauce to a thick consistency by fast boiling, then pour over the meat. Break the eggs, keeping them whole, and slide onto the meat.

Cover the tagine and transfer to the preheated oven. Cook for 10 to 15 minutes, until the whites of the eggs are just set. Serve very hot with flat bread.

KEFTA WITH EGGS

KEFTA AUX OEUFS

This is a Moroccan family dish which makes an ideal supper when served with bread and a green salad. In Tunisia the kefta are cooked in a tomato sauce spiked with harissa. When you are ready to add the eggs, you make little holes in the thick tomato sauce and break the eggs into them. In Morocco, however, simplicity is the key and the kefta are simply cooked in butter and finished with the eggs. The knack is to cook the eggs until the whites have just set but the yolks are still soft – to enjoy this dish to the full you should eat it straight from the tagine, mopping up with hunks of bread the yolk which runs into the buttery sauce.

I was told of an American who so liked this dish in Rabat that he prized the recipe from the street-seller he had eaten it with. Six months later he returned to accuse the street vendor of having left a vital secret out of the recipe – 'however I do it in New York, it just doesn't taste the same' he complained bitterly. 'Ah', said the street vendor, 'that is because you do not have my tagine and my charcoal.' It is true that earthenware does lend a particular flavour to this dish.

500g (1lb) minced beef

2 teaspoons ground cumin

2 teaspoons paprika

¼ teaspoon cayenne pepper

6 tablespoons of finely chopped fresh flat-leaf parsley

3 tablespoons finely chopped fresh coriander

1 onion, peeled and grated

Sea salt

60g (2½oz) butter

4 eggs

Mix the minced beef with the spices, herbs, onion and plenty of salt. Either give a quick whizz in the processor or pound until the paste is very smooth. Dampen your hands and fashion the *kefta* paste into small balls about the size of a marble.

Melt the butter in a tagine or heavy wide casserole over a gentle heat. When the butter has melted add the *kefta* and cook slowly in the butter, turning from time to time, until the *kefta* give off their juice and the buttery sauce in the bottom of the tagine becomes thick. This will take about 20 minutes. When you are ready to eat, break the eggs into the tagine and sprinkle with cayenne pepper. Continue to cook over a gentle heat until the whites of the eggs have set – about 10 minutes. Serve very hot.

ESCABECHE OF PARTRIDGE

LA PERDIZ ESCABECHADA

The ancient technique of cooking in vinegar or escabèche *lends itself as well to small game birds as it does to fish (see recipe page 71). This is another speciality of the Caballo Rojo in Córdoba, whose chef kindly came out of the kitchen to give me his prized recipe. The Spaniards are great hunters and partridge abound both in the hills and on the plains. The Caballo Rojo use the red-legged partridge but the grey-legged, although slightly inferior in flavour, also works well. The birds are first grilled and then simmered in a sauce heavy with vinegar – as the chef explained to me they must take the 'sabor' of the vinegar.*

4 partridges

3 large onions, peeled and chopped into fine half-moons

2 carrots, peeled and chopped into fine rings

4 sprigs fresh thyme

2 sprigs fresh oregano

2 fresh bay leaves

Sea salt

½ teaspoon black peppercorns

100 ml (3½ fl oz) sherry vinegar

1 tablespoon white sugar

100 ml (3½ fl oz) olive oil

Preheat the grill to maximum. Grill the whole partridges for 10 minutes on either side until nicely browned.

Meanwhile, choose a heavy casserole into which all four birds will fit. Place the onions and carrots and remaining ingredients in the casserole and simmer for 10 minutes. Add the grilled birds to the casserole and cook gently for 45 minutes, until the birds are very tender. Serve hot with a few onions and carrots and a little of the sauce.

SPICY LIVER SALAD

SALADE DE FOIE

Salads in Morocco are not just made with vegetables – there are meat and fish salads as well. But the absolute favourite are cooked salads based on offal, particularly lambs' brains. Liver is another popular choice, first marinated in spices, then briefly fried and finally mixed with plenty of very finely chopped coriander, lemon juice and olive oil. The head chef at the Mammounia, the dapper M. Boujemma Mars, told me that the liver should be left just long enough to take up the flavours but never too long before being eaten, or it will become tough and dry. His team of Moroccan women chefs make the liver salad late each afternoon for consumption that evening.

350g (12oz) lamb's liver

2 teaspoons ground cumin

2 teaspoons paprika

Juice of 2 lemons

Groundnut oil

Durum wheat or semolina flour

½ teaspoon coarse sea salt

4 tablespoons finely chopped fresh coriander

4 tablespoons olive oil

Cut the liver into slices 1 cm (½ in) thick. Mix the cumin, paprika and three-quarters of the lemon juice together to form a paste and spread all over the sliced liver. Leave to stand for 2 hours or more.

Cover the base of a frying pan with oil to a depth of 1 cm (½ in) and heat until the oil is hot enough to crisp a cube of bread. Dip a few slices of the liver at a time in the flour and fry briefly until golden brown – no more than 2 minutes. Fry the liver in several batches, taking care never to overcrowd the pan. Remove the liver with a slotted spoon and drain on kitchen paper.

Cut the liver into bite sized pieces – it should still be pink in the middle. Sprinkle with salt, stir in the coriander and finally add the remaining lemon juice and the olive oil. Leave to cool before serving.

PIGEON WITH ALMONDS

PIGEON K'DRA

K'dra *refers to the type of pot in which this style of slowly simmered dish was traditionally cooked over charcoal embers. The k'dra is made of earthenware and tapers from a wide base to a narrower top, with a lid. Pigeons are commonly sold live in the* souks *of Morocco and this is one of the favourite ways of cooking them – if they have escaped the pigeon pie known as pastilla (see page 124 –5) – which is a favourite starter.*

4 squabs or pigeons

Coarse sea salt

90 g (3 oz) whole blanched almonds

125 g (4 oz) unsalted butter

4 large Spanish onions

1 teaspoon saffron strands

Freshly ground black pepper

3 tablespoons chopped fresh coriander

3 tablespoons chopped fresh flat-leaf parsley

1 tablespoon of flaked almonds

Wash the pigeons well inside and out, rubbing them with salt. Pat them dry and place them in a heavy covered pot in which they will just fit. Add the whole almonds and three quarters of the butter.

Grate two of the onions and add them to the pot together with 250 ml (8 fl oz) water. Sprinkle in the saffron strands, a pinch of salt and plenty of pepper. Bring to the boil, turn down to a simmer, cover and leave to cook for 50 minutes, turning the pigeons halfway through cooking.

Finely chop the remaining onions. When the pigeons are very tender, remove from the pot and keep warm. Add the chopped onions and the herbs to the sauce in the pot, cover and cook for 15 minutes until the onions have softened. Meanwhile fry the flaked almonds in the remaining butter.

Check the seasoning of the sauce then pour into the base of a tagine or eathenware serving dish. Arrange the cooked pigeons on top and scatter over the flaked almonds before serving.

RABBIT WITH NUT SAUCE

CONEJO CON PICADA

One of the most distinctive features of Catalan cooking is the picada, *a mixture of nuts, fried bread, saffron, herbs and olive oil used to thicken and flavour sauces. Early cookery books show that the method has been used in Catalonia from the thirteenth century, when the Moors still held some mountain strongholds in the region. Here the* picada *is used to thicken a wine sauce for rabbit, a popular meat with the hunters of Spain, but the recipe applies equally well to chicken and also to monkfish.*

500g (1lb) boneless rabbit

½ teaspoon ground cumin

½ teaspoon freshly ground black pepper

4 tablespoons olive oil

1 tablespoon sherry or white wine vinegar

150ml (5floz) dry sherry or dry white wine

20 blanched almonds

20 blanched hazelnuts

1 slice white bread, crusts removed

2 cloves garlic, peeled

Sea salt

¼ teaspoon saffron strands

2 tablespoons chopped fresh flat-leaf parsley

Cut the rabbit into bite sized pieces and dust with the cumin and pepper. Heat 2 tablespoons of oil in a heavy pan over a high heat and add the rabbit pieces. Fry for 3 minutes, turning regularly, and then add the vinegar. As soon as the vinegar boils add the sherry or wine, bring to the boil, turn down to a simmer, cover and leave to cook for 10 minutes.

Meanwhile make the *picada*. Toast the nuts in a dry frying pan until golden. Fry the bread in a tablespoon of oil until crisp. Pound or process together the nuts, bread, garlic and salt to a smooth paste. Add a little of the juice from the pan to the saffron then add this and the parsley to the paste. Finally add the remaining tablespoon of olive oil. Stir the *picada* into the pan, adding a couple of tablespoons of water to dilute and leave to cook for 10 minutes, until the rabbit is cooked through.

GRAINS, PASTA AND PASTRIES

ABOVE: CARRYING BREAD TO THE OVEN, BHALIL. RIGHT: BRINGING IN THE HARVEST, MOROCCO.

Couscous is perhaps the best known food of North Africa – a pile of steaming grain, served with a spicy broth and some stewed or grilled meats. Those who have been introduced to couscous in Paris, where it is the ultimate cheap late-night food, will expect to find a vegetable stew with raisins and chickpeas, grilled merguez sausages and little pots of spicy *harissa*, in the Algerian manner. But couscous comes in many guises. If you first eat couscous in Tunisia it will probably be served with a fish, usually mullet, and the accompanying stew will be heavily spiked with chilli. The Sicilians of Trapani on the west coast follow the habit of their invaders, and serve their *cuscusu* with a *zuppe de pesce*, the catch of the day cooked in broth with herbs.

Couscous is a durum wheat grain which was a staple element of the diet well before the Arabs arrived in North Africa. It was the Berbers who first introduced the complicated process of making couscous, moulding small grains of semolina which were dried in the sun before being steamed once again. They served the grain with nothing more than butter, accompanied by milk and dates. Today chilled couscous with milk (known as *saycouk*) is still a popular and refreshing family dish, often served with the fresh new broad beans of the spring.

As with so much other Moorish cooking, it is in Morocco that the subtlest variations have developed. There are two principal forms of couscous, the sweet or '*sucré*', as in the classic Fez dish of lamb cooked with dried raisins and caramelized onions (see page 76), and the salt or '*salé*', as in couscous with seven vegetables (see page 112).

Ouarka pastry is one of the great triumphs but also one of the great challenges of Moroccan cooking. Light as a feather, so thin it is almost transparent, it is the key ingredient not just for *pastillas* both sweet and savoury but for *briouats* and *m'hancha*, the classic almond filled pudding also known as 'The snake' (see page 141).

COUSCOUS

Moroccan cooks put more effort into the preparation of the actual couscous than the accompanying sauce. To give an idea of the loving care and attention Moroccan cooks lavish on their couscous, here are the instructions given to me by my friend Oumelktoun.

'Take one kilo of fine couscous and wash it well to remove the starch. Add a little cold water and allow the couscous to soak for 1 minute. Place the couscous in a g'saa, like the one used to make bread, and feel the couscous to open it out with your fingers. Now add a little oil and continue to aerate the couscous with your hands.

Place half a lemon or a tomato in the water in the base of the couscoussier – this will stop it going black. Place the couscoussier over an active fire. Add a little of the couscous to the steamer – it is vital that this first layer of couscous takes the steam before you add the rest. Do not put the top on the steamer and cook the couscous for 3 minutes. Now tip it all out into the g'saa again and moisten it with 1 glass of salt water. Plunge your hands in to feel the grain – it will be very hot but my hands are used to it. Anyway you need to use your hands to tell what the couscous needs, a little more water or not.

After you have felt it for 10 minutes, steam it again for 2 minutes. Again tip it into the g'saa, this time adding a little oil or butter. Handle the couscous well and then return it to the couscoussier. Another 2 minutes steaming and it will be cooked. Arrange it under and over the meat with your hands and then arrange the vegetables over it.

Couscous in Morocco is served in one huge dish, the conical pile of grain concealing the meat, the vegetables artfully propped up against the grain, the delicious broth poured over the whole. It is most often served as a family meal, traditionally on Fridays, the day of rest, when the cook has plenty of time to prepare it and the diners to relax afterwards. For those with rather less time, pre-cooked couscous is a perfectly sensible solution and the packet instructions are very easy to follow. If you do not have a couscoussier, do not worry – a steamer achieves the same effect.

SWEET LAMB COUSCOUS

COUSCOUS T'FAYA

Like sweet tagines, most sweet couscous recipes come from the self-indulgent town of Fez and this well-known version is no exception. The sweetness comes not just from the honey, which is mixed into the sauce, but perhaps more powerfully from the slow-cooked onions and the plump raisins. Serves 6–8.

200g (7oz) dried chickpeas

1 kg (2lb) lamb shoulder, on the bone, cut into 4 pieces, excess fat removed

½ teaspoon freshly ground ginger

1 stick cinnamon

¼ teaspoon saffron

1½ teaspoons freshly ground black pepper

1 small bunch fresh coriander

1 small bunch fresh flat-leaf parsley

8 tablespoons olive oil

1 kg (2lb) large sweet onions

Sea salt

125g (4½oz) dried raisins

1 tablespoon clear honey

1 teaspoon ground cinnamon

500g (1lb) pre-cooked couscous

Soak the chickpeas in plenty of water for 24 hours. Bring a large pan of water to the boil, add the chickpeas and boil hard for 10 minutes then drain.

Place the meat in the bottom of the couscoussier. Add water to the three-quarter level, bring to the boil and skim the scum from the surface. Add the chickpeas, ginger, cinnamon, saffron, ½ teaspoon of the pepper, the herbs tied together in a bunch and 3 tablespoons of the olive oil. Grate 1 onion and add that to the pan. Simmer actively for 1½ hours.

Meanwhile peel the remaining onions and slice into fine half moons. Heat the remaining olive oil in a heavy pan over a low flame, add the onions and leave to cook slowly for 1 hour, stirring occasionally.

When the meat and chickpeas have cooked for 1½ hours add the raisins and salt to the pot. Continue to simmer for another 30 minutes. Meanwhile steam the couscous according to the instructions on the packet. Stir the honey, ground cinnamon and remaining black pepper into the caramelized onions and cook for a further 15 minutes.

Pile the couscous onto a large plate and moisten with plenty of the broth. Remove the meat from the broth, place on the couscous and pile the onion and raisin mixture on top. Serve with additional broth.

COUSCOUS WITH SEVEN VEGETABLES
COUSCOUS AU SEPT LÉGUMES

The vegetables used here are only a suggestion – they can vary according to the season. For example, in spring artichoke hearts, broad beans and peas often find their way into the broth, while in the autumn pumpkins and other squashes are commonly found. But there should always be seven for luck. Remember to adjust cooking times according to the vegetables used. Serves 6–8.

1 kg (2 lb) lamb shoulder, on the bone, cut into 4 pieces, excess fat removed

1 teaspoon ground ginger

1 teaspoon coriander seeds

1 teaspoon freshly ground black pepper

½ teaspoon saffron

4 tablespoons olive oil

1 small bunch fresh coriander

1 small bunch fresh flat-leaf parsley

4 large tomatoes, skinned, cored, seeded and quartered

4 small turnips, peeled and quartered

300 g (11 oz) carrots, peeled and cut into thick strips

300 g (11 oz) white cabbage, quartered and left attached at the base

1 teaspoon sea salt

300 g (11 oz) courgettes, cut into thick strips

300 g (11 oz) aubergine, cut into thick strips

3 small green peppers, cored and cut into quarters

500 g (1 lb) pre-cooked couscous

Place the lamb in the bottom of a couscoussier or double boiler and add sufficient water to come three quarters of the way up the side of the pan. Bring to the boil, skim off the scum which will rise to the surface then add the spices, olive oil, bunch of coriander and parsley tied together with string. Leave to simmer for 45 minutes.

Add the tomatoes, turnips, carrots, cabbage and salt and simmer for a further 30 minutes. Now add the courgettes, aubergine and peppers cover and leave to simmer for 30 minutes. Meanwhile steam the couscous according to the instructions on the packet. Before serving remove the bunch of herbs and check the broth for salt.

KHADIJA'S CHICKEN COUSCOUS

I met Khadija completely by accident and with typical Moroccan hospitality she invited me to join her for a 'vrai couscous' with her delightful family. Although she lives in Fez, Khadija comes from Marrakesh, and she told me this was a Marrakeshi recipe.

I watched as Khadija and her sister Hanane touched the steamed grains of couscous to aerate them, then arranged the couscous in a brightly patterned dish, delicately posing the whole chicken on top and picking out with their fingers each individual vegetable to prop against the chicken, until the whole surface of the couscous was covered. A work of both love and art – and I was delighted to see that the separate bowl of couscous which was prepared for the children received exactly the same degree of attention. Serves 6–8.

150g (5oz) chickpeas, soaked overnight in plenty of water

1.5kg (3½lb) plump chicken

Sea salt

1 large onion, peeled and grated

1 bunch fresh flat-leaf parsley, tied with string

½ teaspoon ground black pepper

1 good pinch saffron

4 tablespoons olive oil

3 glasses water

3 large carrots, peeled

2 large waxy potatoes, peeled

3 courgettes

1 small white cabbage

400g (14oz) slice of pumpkin or other squash

4 tomatoes, peeled and seeded

500g (1lb) pre-cooked couscous

Bring a pan of water to the boil and boil the drained chickpeas hard for 5 minutes. Strain.

Wash the chicken well inside and out with salt. Place it in the bottom of the couscoussier with the grated onion, parsley, pepper, saffron, oil, water and chickpeas. Bring to the boil, cover and leave to simmer for 30 minutes.

Meanwhile prepare the vegetables. Cut the carrots into half across and then into quarters lengthways. Do the same to the potatoes and courgettes. Cut the cabbage into eights, making sure that you leave sufficient base that the pieces do not fall apart. Cut the pumpkin or squash into thick chunks. Roughly chop the tomatoes.

Add the vegetables to the cooking pot, together with a little more water if necessary and a good pinch of salt. Leave to cook for 45 minutes to 1 hour, until the vegetables are very tender. Prepare the couscous according to the instructions on the packet.

BURIED MEAT COUSCOUS

SEFFA MEDFOUNA

This is a ceremonial dish which on special occasions, such as baptisms, is also prepared with pigeons and is traditionally served with glasses of iced milk. The point about it is that the meat is hidden beneath a pile of couscous – which is why it is known as buried meat. When Oumelktoun showed me how to make this ceremonial dish, she was most insistent as to the importance of preparing the couscous properly (see page 110). I am afraid I am a disappointment to Oumelktoun – I tend to use the ready cooked couscous which she considers a travesty. The result is still very good. Serves 6–8

500g (1lb) best quality braising steak

2 onions, peeled and finely chopped

1 stick cinnamon

½ teaspoon of saffron strands

1 teaspoon freshly ground black pepper

Sea salt

2 tablespoons olive oil

1 bunch fresh coriander

½ a bunch fresh flat-leaf parsley

500g (1lb) pre-cooked couscous

100g whole blanched almonds

50g (2oz) butter

Ground cinnamon

Icing sugar

Remove any fat from the beef and cut the meat into bite sized pieces. Place it in a tagine or heavy casserole with the onion, spices, salt to taste, oil and the herbs tied in a bunch. Add sufficient water to just cover and place over a gentle heat. Cook for 1 to 1½ hours, until the meat is tender – the exact time will depend upon the quality of the meat.

Meanwhile steam the couscous according to the instructions on the packet. Fry the almonds in the butter until lightly golden then roughly crush them.

When the meat is cooked remove it from the sauce and keep warm. Boil the sauce down until it is very thick and then strain it. Stir in ¼ teaspoon of ground cinnamon and pour over the meat.

Arrange a layer of couscous on the bottom of a tagine and place the meat in its sauce over it. Sprinkle the crushed almonds over the meat then pile the remaining couscous over it, so that the meat is completely hidden under a conical mound of couscous. Traditionally lines of ground cinnamon and icing sugar are dribbled alternately down the side of couscous, giving a beautiful striped effect.

SICILIAN COUSCOUS WITH FISH STEW

CUSCUSU CON ZUPPA DI PESCE

Couscous is the dish of the day in western Sicily, particularly around the fishing port of Trapani, which looks across to the Egadi Islands and beyond them to Tunisia. To enjoy cuscusu *at its best I was directed to a small and unprepossessing looking restaurant right by the hoverfoil departure point for the largest of the islands, Favignana. There was no choice – the meal started with a selection of antipasti which bore a remarkable similarity to those that might have been found across the water in Africa and followed up with a steaming pile of couscous and a fish stew with the catch of the day. It was delicious, especially when rounded off with the classic North African pudding of orange salad. Serves 6.*

2 kg (4½ lb) mixed fish, such as grey and red mullet, sea bream

1 onion, peeled and finely chopped

2 cloves garlic, peeled and finely chopped

6 tablespoons olive oil

4 tomatoes, peeled, seeded and finely chopped

4 tablespoons finely chopped flat-leaf parsley

Sea salt

¼ teaspoon Cayenne pepper

500 g (1 lb) pre-cooked couscous

1 litre (1¾ pints) water

Wash the fish well and if they are large cut them into slices. It is important that the fish pieces should be of roughly equal size, so that they cook evenly.

Put the onion, garlic and oil in the base of a couscoussier or pot over which a steamer will fit. Place over a moderate heat and cook for 15 minutes, stirring occasionally, until the onion is soft. Add the tomatoes, parsley, salt and cayenne pepper and cook for a further 15 minutes until you have a thick sauce. Meanwhile moisten the couscous according to the instructions on the packet.

Add the water to the tomato sauce together with the fish pieces. Place the couscous in the steamer above and leave all to cook for 10 minutes, until the fish is ready. Fluff up the couscous with a fork, dribble with olive oil if you like and serve the fish stew on the side.

TUNISIAN FISH COUSCOUS

COUSCOUS DE POISSON

In Tunisia couscous is often served with fish, usually mullet. Unlike the gently spiced broths which accompany couscous in Morocco, the accompanying stew is hot with chilli. The fish is cooked with vegetables to produce a real fisherman's dish, cooked in an hour in one pot with the couscous steaming above it. If the idea of cooking the initial stage with the fish head horrifies you, or bones worry you, simply use fish stock instead of water and buy fish fillets instead of a whole fish. Serves 6.

1 kg (2 lb) whole firm white fish such as grey mullet, sea bream, sea bass cut into 6 pieces

1 large onion, quartered

3 stick celery, chopped

2 large carrots, cut into eighths

3 small turnips, quartered

2 large tomatoes, quartered

2 large dried red chillies

6 tablespoons olive oil

2 cloves garlic, finely chopped

¼ teaspoon saffron

1½ litres (2½ pints) water or fish stock

Sea salt and freshly ground black pepper

500 g (1 lb) pre-cooked couscous

A pinch of cayenne

½ teaspoon paprika

1 tablespoon chopped fresh coriander

Harissa (see page 155)

Roughly chop the chillies. Heat 2 tablespoons of the oil together with the chillies and garlic in a large heavy pan with a lid, placed over a gentle heat. As soon as the chillies and garlic start to sizzle, add the saffron, onion, carrot and turnip. Stir together then pour in the water (or fish stock if you are using it). Bring gently to the boil, then turn down to a simmer. Skim any scum from the surface, add salt and plenty of pepper, cover and leave to simmer for 30 minutes.

Add the tomatoes. Cook for a further 15 minutes. Meanwhile prepare the couscous according to the packet instructions.

After the stew has been cooking for 45 minutes, gently slip in the fish pieces. These will need to cook for 10 minutes, during which time you should also steam the couscous, over the stew if you have a couscoussier, or alternatively in a separate container.

Remove the couscous and fluff it up with a fork. Mix the cayenne pepper and paprika into the remaining olive oil and dribble over the surface of the couscous. Sprinkle the coriander over the fish stew and serve with *harissa*.

MOORS AND CHRISTIANS
MOROS Y CRISTIANOS

*A ring of buttered, herby rice surrounds a pile of garlicky black beans, the white rice being the
Christians and the black beans the Moors. A piece of simple imagery which reflects a long
period of religious and social conflict. Many towns in the south and east of Spain still enact
pageants to represent the final expulsion of the invaders but this dish, with its beans cooked in
Mexican style, must post date that belated departure. What is true is that the surrounding circle
of rice owes its being to the irrigation systems which the Arabs revived, allowing the
development of the paddy fields. The best rice in Spain comes from the Valencia region, which it
is no surprise to discover, is also the home of paella.*

300g (11oz) black beans

2 Spanish onions, peeled

6 cloves garlic, peeled

1 teaspoon freshly ground black
pepper

4 rashers smoked streaky bacon

2 tablespoons olive oil

2 teaspoons paprika

1 teaspoon ground cumin

1 slice day old white bread

60g (2½oz) butter

300g (11oz) short grain rice

750ml (1¼ pints) chicken stock

2 fresh bay leaves

A sprig each of fresh rosemary and
thyme

Soak the beans in plenty of water overnight. Drain
the beans and rinse well. Place them in a heavy
lidded casserole and pour over enough water to
cover by 2.5cm (1in). Cut one of the onions in half,
making sure that it is still attached at the stalk so
that it does not fall apart, and push it into the centre
of the beans. Add 2 of the peeled whole garlic cloves
and half the pepper. Bring to the boil, boil hard for 5
minutes, then turn down to a simmer. Cover and
leave to cook for 45 minutes.

Finely chop the whole onion and the garlic cloves.
Dice the bacon, including the fat. Put the olive oil in
a heavy frying pan over a medium heat and add the
chopped onion, garlic and bacon. Cook for 20
minutes, stirring regularly, until the onion is very soft
and the bacon fat has run. Now add the paprika,
cumin and remaining pepper to the pan and stir
well. Tear the bread into small pieces and after 2
minutes add it to the pan. Cook, stirring, for another
2 minutes then remove from the heat.

When the beans have cooked for 45 minutes, remove the half onion and, if necessary, stir in enough water to just cover. Stir in the onion, garlic and bacon mixture and a pinch of salt (careful as the bacon is salty). Cover and leave to simmer for a further 45 minutes, or until the beans are just tender. Stir occasionally, to prevent sticking, and add a little more water if necessary – the beans should have little sauce when finished.

Prepare the rice. Melt two thirds of the butter in a heavy deep non-stick frying pan which will fit in your oven. Finely chop the remaining half onion and add it to the melted butter. Sweat gently over a low heat for 15 minutes, until the onion is soft but not coloured.

Meanwhile heat the stock to boiling point and preheat the oven to 150°C/300°F/gas mark 2.

Add the rice to the frying pan and turn in the fat to make sure the grains are coated. Pour over the hot stock, tuck in the herbs and leave to cook over a moderate heat for 15 minutes. Do not stir the rice or it will turn sticky. At the end of the cooking period the rice should have absorbed all the liquid; dot the surface with the remaining butter and transfer the pan to the preheated oven for 5 minutes. Remove and leave to stand for 10 minutes. To serve, arrange a pile of beans in the middle of each plate and surround with a ring of rice.

PASTA WITH SARDINES
PASTA CON LE SARDE

In 827 Euphemius sailed from Kairouen (now Tunisia) with an army of 10,000 Saracens to take Sicily. He established his beachhead on the western tip of the island, at Mazaro del Vallo, and, so the story goes, sent his soldiers out to forage the hillsides for food. They found stalks of wild fennel, dried raisins from the vines, pine nuts from the trees which ringed the coast and sardines from the sea. They already had the pasta which some historians claim the Arabs brought to Italy and the saffron which they had introduced to Spain so they put all the ingredients together to make what has become the national dish of Sicily. A romantic fiction, but one which enhanced my pleasure when I first ate pasta con le sarde *in the crumbling city of Palermo. A truly medieval touch is the sprinkling of spiced breadcrumbs .*

250g (9oz) fennel, including stalks and the feathery fronds

Sea salt

1 large onion, peeled and chopped

150ml (5floz) olive oil

2 tablespoons pine nuts

2 tablespoons dried currants

4 fresh sardines, filleted

A few gratings of nutmeg

Freshly ground black pepper

90–125g (3½-4½oz) per head of dried bucatini

SPICED BREADCRUMBS

2 slices of dry white country bread, crusts removed

½ teaspoon ground cinnamon

¼ teaspoon ground nutmeg

¼ teaspoon finely ground black pepper

A good pinch of sea salt

2 tablespoons olive oil

Bring a large pot of salted water to the boil, add the fennel and simmer for 15 minutes, until tender. Remove the fennel and reserve the water for cooking the pasta. Roughly chop the cooked fennel.

Cook the onion in the olive oil for 6 to 8 minutes, until soft and golden. Add the chopped fennel, the pine nuts and currants, the sardine fillets and the nutmeg and plenty of pepper. Moisten with 4 tablespoons of the fennel water. Cook the sauce for 15 minutes, stirring regularly. Add a little more fennel water if necessary (but be careful – it is salty).The fish should fall apart.

Meanwhile prepare the spiced breadcrumbs. Crumble the bread with your fingers and mix in the spices and salt. Heat the oil and when hot add the spiced crumbs. Fry quickly, until golden brown.

Bring the fennel water back to the boil and add the bucatini. Cook the pasta for 8 to 10 minutes, until tender. Drain the pasta, mix in with the sauce and serve with the spiced crumbs on the side.

PASTA WITH FISH
FIDEUÀ

Colman Andrews, in his splendid work Catalan Cuisine, *argues that the unique Catalan pasta known as* fideus *has an Arabic origin from the word* fada *or to overflow and that* fideus *turns up in a Catalan cookery book from 1429. What is interesting about this pasta dish is that is cooked in exactly the same way as paella, that is simply put in the pan and left to absorb the liquid. It is difficult to get hold of* fideus *pasta outside of Spain but I have had perfectly good results with spaghettini broken into short lengths. On no account use egg pasta.*

4 tablespoons olive oil

375g (13oz) monkfish fillet, cut into 5cm (2in) pieces

250g (9oz) uncooked prawns in the shell

500g (1lb) medium sized clams

1 litre (1¾ pints) fish stock

4 cloves garlic, peeled and finely chopped

2 large beef tomatoes, peeled, seeded and chopped

½ teaspoon saffron strands

1 teaspoon paprika

Sea salt

300g (11oz) spaghettini

Put the oil in a heavy deep-sided pan (or better still a paella pan) over a high heat. Briefly fry the monkfish until lightly browned and lift out with a slotted spoon. Do the same with the prawns until they just take colour and again remove. Set both monkfish and prawns aside. Scrub the clams and put them in a large bowl of heavily salted water. Put the stock on to simmer.

Add the chopped garlic to the oil in the pan and as soon as the garlic starts to sizzle add the tomatoes, saffron, paprika and salt to taste. Cook for 5 minutes, stirring occasionally, until the tomatoes break down. Break the spaghettini into 5cm (2in) lengths directly into the pan and turn in the sauce to coat. Add the pieces of monkfish and pour over the hot stock. Bring to the boil then turn the heat down so that the stock simmers actively. Leave to cook for 20 minutes then add the clams and the prawns. Cook for a further 10 minutes, by which time the liquid should all have been absorbed by the pasta – if necessary turn up the heat to reduce the remains of liquid.

Meanwhile preheat the grill to maximum. When the pasta is ready, transfer the pan under the grill for 2 minutes. Brown the surface lightly and serve.

OUARKA PASTRY

Making *ouarka*, like so much else in Moroccan cooking, is traditionally the preserve of the women, particularly those from the very south of the country. At the Centre de Formation en Cuisine Traditionelle, a centre set up by His Majesty the King within the walls of the palace compound in Rabat to train girls from poorer families as cooks, I watched *ouarka* being prepared by a cook who made the process look deceptively simple, but as the head teacher, Mlle Boukra, told me, 'months of practice are not enough'.

First a simple paste of fine flour, salt and water is made. The paste is worked until 'when you make to let it fall from your hand then recatch it, the pastry follows the movement of your hand'. The pastry is then left to rest in an earthenware dish with a little water poured around it.

If this sounds tricky, the next stage is nothing less than astounding. A circular, wide, thin based, shallow-sided pan made especially for the purpose is turned upside down over heat. The cook picks up a small ball of the dough and in a repeated circular motion dabs it against the heated surface, each time leaving a little of the pastry against the surface. This process is aided by a second woman who with her fingers smooths together the dabs. When the surface of the pan is covered with dabs (which takes about thirty seconds) the circle of pastry is gently lifted off from one edge with the fingers. Each leaf is put to rest under a damp cloth. Then the process starts all over again – and is repeated hundreds of times.

Apparently some male chefs in Morocco have now learnt the art of making *ouarka* but according to Mlle Boukra 'they work astoundingly quickly but the pastry does not have the same calmness'. My own attempts to make *ouarka* have not resulted in anything approaching a state of calm and I do not advise you to try it. It is a true work of art which is best appreciated by the eye, and later the palate, rather than the hand.

Most cooks in Morocco buy ready made *ouarka* leaves (or even ready made *pastilla*), but elsewhere they are not easily available and you will probably have to substitute strudel or filo pastry. Spring roll leaves also work well.

PIGEON PIE
PASTILLA

This elaborate pie demonstrates the manner in which the different culinary influences in Morocco became intermingled early on to produce a distinctive and elaborate result.

Fat pigeons poached in a liquid rich with butter and the saffron brought by the Moors to Andalucia form one layer in the crispy pastry which the Arabs learnt to make from the Persians. Next comes a layer of eggs curdled in the lightly spiced poaching stock, probably thought up by the court cooks of al-Andaluz for added richness. And then a layer of sweetened almond paste, almost indispensable in any pastry, sweet or savoury, cooked by the Moors in Spain. A final criss-crossing of cinnamon in the traditional manner and the pastilla *was ready.*

Today it is served as a starter throughout Morocco, though for western kitchens it is better suited as a main course. The most classic version is still made with pigeons but also often with small chickens. New variants include seafood, and I have also had a very light sweet pastilla *filled with thickened milk and crunchy almonds. Traditionally,* pastilla *made with ouarka pastry is always fried, but this is more difficult with filo pastry. Some smart Moroccan restaurants now bake* pastilla *in the oven in deference to lighter modern tastes and this simpler method is the one I use. Serves 6–8.*

3 x 400g (14oz) squab pigeons or spring chickens

4 sprigs each fresh parsley and coriander, tied into a bunch

1 stick cinnamon

½ teaspoon black pepper

A good pinch of sea salt

1 onion, peeled and grated

200g (7oz) unsalted butter

200g (7oz) whole blanched almonds

Ground cinnamon

2 tablespoons icing sugar

4 whole eggs

Yolks of 4 eggs

500g (1lb) filo pastry

Place the pigeons breast side down in a heavy pan in which they will just fit. Add the herbs, cinnamon, pepper, salt, grated onion and 60g (2½oz) of butter. Pour sufficient water to just cover the pigeons. Bring to the boil, turn down to a slow simmer, cover and leave to cook for 1¼ hours.

Gently fry the whole almonds in 25g (1oz) of butter until golden brown. When the almonds are cool grind them coarsely. Sift together 1 teaspoon ground cinnamon and two thirds of the icing sugar and mix thoroughly into the almonds.

Remove the cooked pigeons from the pan and leave to cool. Reduce the poaching liquid to half its volume then leave to cool. Beat the eggs and yolks until they are frothy. Stir the beaten eggs into the broth. Return the pan to the lowest heat and stir constantly for 5 minutes, until the mixture thickens to produce a thick sauce. Check the seasoning.

Remove the skin from the birds and with your fingers shred the flesh, discarding all the bones. Preheat the oven to 180°C/350°C/gas mark 4.

Melt the remaining butter over a low heat and skim off the scum. Lightly grease a non stick shallow round pie tin. Lay a sheet of filo across it, letting the edges hang over, and brush lightly with melted butter. Lay another sheet at a 60° angle and again brush the surface with butter. Repeat with another 4 sheets of filo, until the surface of the pie dish is completely covered and the circle is complete.

Scatter the shredded pigeon over the pastry and top with the egg sauce. Fold two layers of filo in half and place in the preheated oven for 1 minute, to crisp up. Place these over the egg sauce and top with the almond, cinnamon and sugar mixture. Fold in the overlapping edges of filo, brushing the surface lightly with butter. Now lay two sheets of filo over the surface and gently tuck them under the base, cutting off any excess. Brush the surface with melted butter and pour remaining butter around the edges of the tin.

Bake in the preheated oven for 30 minutes then carefully invert the pie onto a baking sheet. Bake it upside down for a further 20 minutes. Return to top side up. Bake for a further 10 minutes, until the top is crispy golden. Sprinkle the surface with cinnamon and icing and serve absolutely piping hot.

BRIK À L'OEUF AND BRIOUATS

The favourite snack food of Tunisia.

200g (7oz) tuna preserved in olive oil

Sea salt and freshly ground black pepper

2 tablespoons finely chopped flat-leaf parsley

Juice of ½ a lemon

4 leaves of filo pastry

4 small eggs

Sunflower oil for frying

Drain the tuna from the oil and mix with plenty of seasoning, the parsley and the lemon juice. Place the frying oil in a wide non-stick pan and heat until the oil is nearly smoking. Use the outer rim of a large plate to cut a circle from each sheet of filo pastry.

Take one circle of pastry, place a tablespoon of the tuna mixture in the middle and break the egg over the top. Rapidly fold the pastry into a half moon shape and slip into the hot oil. Cook for 45 seconds on one side, until golden brown, then turn over and cook for a further 30 seconds. Drain each circle on kitchen paper and serve very hot.

TO MAKE THE BRIOUATS

Briouats *can come in three shapes – triangles, squares or cylinders. I prefer cylinders for the kefta and rice fillings.*

Filo pastry (you can also use spring roll leaves)

Groundnut or sunflower oil

Take a sheet of filo pastry 15cm x 10cm (6in x 4 in). Place 1½ teaspoons of filling across the bottom, 2.5cm (1in) in from either edge and from the base. Fold in each edge lengthways so that you have a strip 5cm (2in) wide and then roll up the *briouat* so you have a cylinder. Place under a damp tea-towel until you are ready to cook.

Fill a pan with the frying oil to a depth of 5cm (2 in). When the oil is hot fry the *briouats* a few at a time until they crisp and golden. Never overcrowd the pan. Sprinkle with icing sugar and serve very hot.

KEFTA FILLING FOR BRIOUATS

250g (9oz) very finely minced lamb

2 teaspoons ground cinnamon

1 teaspoon freshly ground black pepper

1 teaspoon sea salt

1 tablespoon very finely chopped flat leaf parsley

25g (1oz) butter

2 eggs, beaten

1 egg yolk, beaten

Mix into the meat the cinnamon, pepper, salt and parsley. Melt the butter in a heavy pan and fry the meat for 3 to 4 minutes, stirring constantly. Now slowly add the egg mixture to the meat, still stirring. When you have added all the egg, cook for a further 2 minutes, stirring. Take off the heat and leave to cool.

RICE FILLING FOR BRIOUATS

This filling is quite frankly extraordinary and may not be to western tastes, especially as briouats *with rice are served as a starter, not the pudding that might have been expected. It has a flavour of long ago, of a time when the rich enjoyed heavily scented sweetmeats such as this, and has survived to remain one of the most popular fillings for* briouats *in Morocco today.*

100g (4oz) long-grain rice

300ml (10floz) full-cream milk

3 tablespoons water

50g (2oz) butter

A pinch of salt

4 teaspoons icing sugar

2 teaspoons orange flower water

50g (2oz) whole almonds

Rinse the rice very well. Heat the milk with the water, half the butter and a good pinch of salt, taking care that it does not boil over. Add the rice and cook covered over a gentle heat for 10 minutes, by which time the rice should have absorbed all the liquid. Stir in the sugar and orange-flower water, take off the heat and leave covered.

Fry the almonds in the remaining butter until crisp and golden. As soon as they are cool enough to handle, chop them finely. Stir into the cooled rice.

SWEETS AND DRINKS

ABOVE: JEWEL-LIKE POMEGRANATE SEEDS RIGHT: DRIED FIGS FOR SALE IN MARRAKESH.

The concept of pudding does not really exist in Morocco. That is not to say that there are not sweet dishes – from the salads through to the tagines there is more often than not a hint of sugar mixed with the spice. As in medieval times, there is no fear of combining sweet with savoury. For ceremonial occasion there is the sweet couscous *seffa* – a pile of grain dressed with butter, sugar and cinnamon, served with a glass of creamy ice-cold milk – and *pastillas* – thin layers of *ouarka* pastry crisped in oil, layered with crushed almonds, topped with a milk cream scented with orange flower water.

In typical family homes, the meal is always rounded off with a bowl of fruit, preferably served on ice, to refresh the palate. For special occasions the fruit may be cooked in honey and spice, stuffed with nuts and butter or simply dressed with perfumed waters and cinnamon – as in the classic orange salad. It is these fruit based dishes which I love best, which seem to me the best way to finish a rich meal, and for which I have collected recipes not just in Morocco but in Spain, Provence and Italy.

But the Arabs did introduce the sugar cane which allowed the confection of the sweet sticky pastries and puddings, of which today the people of the southern Mediterranean are so fond. Pastries and biscuits do still abound, to be enjoyed with a cup of sweet mint tea or strong black coffee. I defy anyone to pop in on the briefest errand to a household in Morocco and escape without something to drink and these sweetmeats to nibble.

ORANGE SALAD WITH CINNAMON

ORANGES À LA CANNELLE

This is the classic pudding in Moroccan restaurants. The mixture of sharp and sweet flavours acts as a perfect palate cleanser from the rich tagines which precede it. Similar orange salads are popular from Spain to Sicily (where the orange flower water is sometimes replaced by the even more heavily scented jasmine water).

6 large oranges

4 teaspoons orange flower water

4 teaspoons icing sugar

1 teaspoon ground cinnamon

2 sprigs fresh mint

Peel the oranges, making sure you remove the pith. Cut the oranges across into fine rounds, remove any pips and arrange the rounds on a circular plate. Pour over the orange flower water and dredge with the sugar and half the cinnamon. Chill well before serving sprinkled with the remaining cinnamon and decorated with the sprigs of mint.

MELON SALAD WITH ROSE-WATER

SALADE DE MELONS À L'EAU DE ROSE

The fruit of the desert, melons have always been much prized in Arabic culture. In season in Morocco they are sold by the barrow-load and, to quench your thirst, street-sellers have slices of watermelon to be consumed on the spot. This gaily coloured salad scented with rose-water and topped with nuts makes them even more exotic.

½ a large or 1 small yellow melon

¼ of a watermelon

1 tablespoon white sugar

4 teaspoons rose-water

2 teaspoons flaked toasted pistachio nuts or almonds

Scoop out the seeds from the yellow melon, cut the flesh off the rind and then into bite sized pieces. Cut the flesh of the watermelon off the rind, pick out the seeds and again cut the flesh into bite sized pieces. Combine the two melons, sprinkle with the sugar and rose-water and leave to macerate in the fridge for 2 hours. Serve very cold, sprinkled with the nuts.

FRUIT SALAD WITH ORANGE FLOWER WATER

SALADE DE FRUITS À L'EAU DE FLEUR D'ORANGER

Morocco does not grow just exotic fruits designed for hot weather – in the autumn the roads of the High and Middle Atlas are lined with small boys sitting in front of their buckets of apples, pears and plums, hoping to attract a passing sale. These harder fruits make an excellent fruit salad, which should be served in a slightly soupy manner with plenty of liquid.

3 apples

3 pears

4 plums

Juice of 2 oranges

Juice of 2 lemons

2 tablespoons of white sugar

2 teaspoons runny honey

8 teaspoons orange flower water

2 sprigs fresh mint

Peel the fruit and cut the flesh into dice. Beat together the orange and lemon juice, sugar and honey and pour over the fruit. Leave to macerate for 2 hours and sprinkle over the orange flower water just before serving.

STUFFED BAKED APRICOTS

ABRICOTS FOURRÉS AUX AMANDES

Some of the sweetest apricots in the Mediterranean come from Provence, which is where I picked up this recipe.

500g (1 lb) apricots

90g (3½oz) ground almonds

90g (3½oz) caster sugar

1 egg yolk

1 teaspoon ground cinnamon

2 teaspoons rose-water

Halve the apricots lengthways and remove the stone. Preheat the oven to 200°C/400°F/gas mark 6.

Mix together the remaining ingredients. Stuff a kernel of the mixture into each halved apricot and place in an earthenware baking dish. Bake for 15 to 20 minutes, until the stuffing is lightly browned on top, and serve warm.

PEARS IN HONEY AND SAFFRON

PERAS ESTOFADOS

Although the Moors introduced sugar cane to Spain, their most luxurious desserts were often made with the scented local honeys which had become popular in Roman times. Today honey and nut sweets are still widely found and honey is also used to cook fruits. The saffron added to this syrup for pears gives the fruit a glorious golden colour as well as adding to the honey scent.

4 firm pears

2 heaped tablespoons honey

Juice of 1 lemon

250 ml (8 fl oz) water

1 stick cinnamon

2 cloves

¼ teaspoon saffron strands

Peel the pears, leaving the stalks intact. Put the honey and lemon juice in a heavy-bottomed pan into which the pears will fit snugly and place over a moderate heat. Stir until the honey has melted then add the water and spices. Keep stirring until the liquid comes to the boil then turn down the heat and leave to simmer for 5 minutes. Now add the pears to the liquid and simmer for 20 minutes, turning carefully halfway through and basting the pears regularly with the sauce. Leave the pears to cool in the syrup before serving.

STUFFED DATES

DATTES FOURRÉES

Buying dates in Morocco is a complicated business. You must be prepared to enter into a discussion not just of price but of provenance, age and quality, then to taste from various gleaming piles and only finally to haggle over quantity and volume, probably by this time over a glass of mint tea. In vain will you protest that you only want a few dates to nibble at on the journey – the staple food of the desert must be treated with true reverence. You may even be dragged into which oasis or palmeraie begets the best dates, or at least the sins of other producers. Which is why for sweetmeats dates are stuffed with the most expensive nut of all, pistachio. If you cannot get unsalted pistachios, increase the quantity of ground almonds to replace them.

16 fresh dates

3 tablespoons ground almonds

2 tablespoons finely chopped unsalted pistachio nuts

2 tablespoons caster sugar

50g (2oz) unsalted butter, at room temperature

With a sharp knife, make a slit down the centre of each date and carefully remove the stone. In the food processor mix together the almonds, pistachio nuts, sugar and butter, adding a very little water so that you have a smooth paste. Fashion the paste into nuggets the size of date stones and use these to stuff the dates. Chill well before serving.

LEMON WATER ICE

GRANITA DI LIMONE

The Arabs used to bring down the snows from Etna to make their cooling shar'bats, long iced drinks based on fruit and sugar syrup. The water ices or granitas for which the island is famous are based on the same principle. Always remove a granita from the freezer 30 minutes before serving.

175g (6oz) caster sugar
300ml (10floz) water
Juice of 6 lemons, strained

Mix together the sugar and water. Bring to the boil and simmer uncovered for 5 minutes. Leave the syrup to cool. Stir the lemon juice into the syrup. Place in the freezer and stir every 15 minutes for 2 hours, then every 30 minutes for a further hour, or until the granita has nearly frozen solid but still has a slightly slushy consistency.

WATERMELON GRANITA

GRANITA DI COCOMERO

The perfumed flower water and aromatic spice add a particularly Arab flavour to this beautiful pale pink granita.

1kg (2lb) slice watermelon
250g (9oz) caster sugar
150ml (5floz) water
Juice of ½ lemon
1 tablespoon orange flower water
½ teaspoon ground cinnamon

Remove the seeds and rind of the melon and process the flesh until you have a smooth purée. Bring the sugar and water to the boil. Simmer for 5 minutes then take off the heat. When cool, stir in the lemon juice, orange flower water and cinnamon. Combine the syrup with the watermelon purée. Pour into a mould and place in the freezer. Stir every 15 minutes for 2 hours, then every 30 minutes for a further hour, or until the granita has nearly frozen solid but still has a slightly slushy consistency.

ALMOND ICE-CREAM

HELADO DE ALMENDRA

It wasn't just in Sicily that the Moors taught the art of making water ices – they also used the snows in Spain, particularly from the Sierra Nevada, the mountains which provide the backdrop to the Alhambra in Granada. This was the sort of ice that I fantasize the ladies of the court might have enjoyed, sitting in their filigree cages beside the water-filled gardens of the Generalife, able to look over to the white washed town on the opposite hillside but never to visit it.

150g (5oz) white sugar

500ml (17floz) water

Finely grated zest of 1 unwaxed lemon

1 stick cinnamon

200g (7oz) finely ground blanched almonds

Mix together the sugar, water and lemon zest, add the cinnamon stick and bring to the boil. Take off the heat and leave to infuse for 30 minutes. Bring back to the boil, stir in the almonds and again take immediately off the heat. Freeze, stirring and beating every 30 minutes, for 2 hours and then every hour for the next 2 hours (or use an ice-cream maker).

BLANCMANGE

MANJAR BLANCO

The Arabic pudding mulhalabya *is known to the English as blancmange, source of a thousand school day nightmares. Yet it was a favourite medieval pudding and one which remains popular today both in Spain and Morocco. Fortunately, the lightly set milk cream is a long way from those horrific memories. I prefer to use both rice and cornflour but if you find rice flour difficult to obtain then cornflour alone will do – simply slightly reduce the overall quantities of flour.*

In Spain the pudding is normally sprinkled with crushed fried almonds but I also like the classic Arabic topping of slivers of pistachio. I do though draw the line at silver leaf.

90g (3½oz) rice flour

25g (1oz) cornflour

1 litre (1¾ pints) full cream milk

90g (3½oz) white sugar

Zest of ½ a lemon, preferably unwaxed

1 stick cinnamon

75g (3oz) ground almonds

16 whole almonds

25g (1oz) butter

Ground cinnamon

Mix together the rice flour and cornflour and slowly stir in 150ml (5floz) of the milk, until you have a smooth cream. Put the remaining milk, sugar, lemon zest and cinnamon stick in a heavy pan and place over a low heat until warm. Add the flour, cream and the ground almonds and heat very gently, stirring all the time with a wooden spoon, until the cream is just thick enough to coat the back of the spoon – around 15 minutes. Take off the heat, remove the cinnamon stick and lemon zest and spoon into four individual serving dishes. Leave to cool.

Fry the whole almonds in the butter until browned, pat dry and then crush lightly. As soon as the blancmange starts to form a skin, sprinkle the surface with the crushed almonds and plenty of cinnamon. Chill well before serving.

PASTRIES

The Moors loved sugar and nuts and nowhere can this be seen more clearly than in the pastries which they nurtured and which can still be found all around the Mediterranean. I don't think I have ever felt so close to the time of al-Andaluz as when I once struggled sweating to the top of the kasbah in Tangier and sat looking out across the straits to Spain, sipping at my scalding mint tea and nibbling on sugar soaked pastries stuffed with almonds and pistachios.

There are literally hundreds of different types of pastries, with many regional and local variations. Many of them are best left in the hands of the skilled *pâtissier* – a sentiment evidently shared by the Fourth Marquis of Bute when he was preparing his labour of love, *Moorish Recipes* (sadly he died before it was published in the 1950s). On the subject of *Ktaif*, a speciality of Tetuan, he remarks:

'This is probably the most difficult to prepare and takes the longest time to make of all the dishes here given, and however pleasing to the taste, is by no means the most attractive to the eye.'

GAZELLES' HORNS
CORNES DE GAZELLE

Shaped into little crescents said to reassemble the horns of the gazelles that once roamed the Atlas mountains, drenched in sugar and scented perfume, boasting the lightest pastry, made with orange flower water and concealing a rich almond filling, these exquisite pastries are from a bygone era. But if making m'hanncha *is fiddly, making* cornes de gazelle *is downright difficult. This was a recipe for rich households with plenty of servants, their wealth reflected in the amount of orange flower water needed. The problem is the pastry, which is made from a virtually fatless dough that needs to be worked and kneaded and stretched to reach the right degree of thinness. It is not something to do in a hurry or when you are feeling already stressed.*

MAKES ABOUT 20 PASTRIES

150g (5½oz) ground almonds

75g (3oz) icing sugar

½ teaspoon ground cinnamon

1 medium egg, beaten

Orange flower water

225g (8oz) plain white flour

1 tablespoon melted unsalted butter

A pinch of salt

Sieve together the almonds, icing sugar and cinnamon. Add the egg and a teaspoon of orange flower water. Mix well together until you have a paste. Chill.

Make a well in the centre of the sieved flour and add the melted butter and the salt. A little at a time, add orange flower water, stirring all the time with a wooden spoon. You should add just enough to make a smooth dough – about 4 to 5 tablespoons. Work the dough very well with your hands for 20 minutes, until it is smooth and elastic.

Preheat the oven to 180°C/350°F/gas mark 4. Lightly grease a wooden board and a rolling pin with butter. Separate the dough into two balls and roll one out until it is very thin, turning the dough onto the rolling pin and also rotating the board. Take teaspoons of the almond paste and arrange at 3–4 cm (1¼–1½in) intervals down the length of the pastry, just in from the edge. Take the edge of the pastry and carefully stretch it outwards then fold over the mounds of paste. Cut out with a pastry cutter, pinch the edges together and fashion into a crescent shape. Prick each pastry several times with a thick needle. Place on a buttered oven tray and repeat until all the pastry and almond paste is used up – you should have about 20 little pastries in all.

Bake in the preheated oven for 15 minutes – the pastries must not brown, only take on the slightest fleck of gold. Take them from the oven and sprinkle orange flower water and icing sugar over them while still warm. Leave to cool before serving.

'THE SNAKE'

M'HANNCHA

This is the most famous pastry of Morocco, a gleaming coil of crisp buttery pastry stuffed with a rich almond filling scented with orange flower water and cinnamon. It looks beautiful, tastes wonderful but it is fiddly and expensive to prepare. In Morocco it can be bought from the local pâtissier. *I make it using filo pastry rather than the* ouarka *which would be traditional, and it is worth the effort for a special occasion.*

100g (4oz) whole almonds

300g (11oz) ground almonds

50g (2oz) icing sugar

100g (4oz) caster sugar

125g (4½oz) unsalted butter, softened

1 teaspoon ground cinnamon

2 teaspoons orange flower water (you could also use rose-water)

Filo pastry

1 egg yolk

Fry the whole almonds in a knob of the butter until golden brown on both sides – take care they do not burn. Either process them or pound them in a pestle and mortar until you have a slightly crunchy texture. Mix into the ground almonds and add the two sugars, 100g (4oz) of the butter, the cinnamon and orange flower water. With your hands form to a smooth paste and chill for 30 minutes. Preheat the oven to 180°C/350°F/gas mark 4.

Take two sheets of filo pastry and glue them together end to end with a little of the egg yolk. Roll out the almond paste to a tube the thickness of your thumb and lay it the length of the filo pastry. Roll the pastry up so that you have a long tube. Repeat this process until all the almond paste is used.

Fashion one of the tubes of filled pastry into a coil, starting from the centre. Use egg yolk to stick the ends of pastry together and repeat with the remaining rolls until you have a large coil or 'snake'. Place on a buttered baking tray. Melt the remaining butter and brush this over the surface of the pastry.

Bake in the preheated oven for 25 to 30 minutes, until lightly browned. Leave to cool before serving.

CONVENT SWEETS

It may seem unlikely, but after the Arabs were pushed from their invaded lands, it was the convents who largely took up the tradition of sweet-making. In the area around Jérez, the nuns became especially skilled at sweet-making because of the number of egg yolks they received. The whites were needed to clarify the wine of Jérez, from the Persian shiraz – sherry as we know it – and the yolks had to be put to some use. Today in Seville there are cooperatives which gather sweets for sale from the various convents around the region and convent sweets are found all over Spain and Portugal.

PINE NUT AND ALMOND ROLLS

MAKES ABOUT 12
250 g (9 oz) white sugar
150 ml (5 fl oz) water
½ a vanilla pod
Juice of ¼ a lemon
100 g (4 oz) whole blanched almonds
200 g (7 oz) pine nuts
1 egg yolk

Put the sugar, water, vanilla and lemon juice in a small heavy pan and place over a fierce heat. When the sugar has melted turn the heat down to medium and leave to simmer for 15 minutes.

Meanwhile combine the almonds with half the pine nuts. Either pound in a pestle and mortar or give a quick turn in the processor until you have a slightly knobbly paste. Add the egg yolk to the paste and stir in well. Now add 2 teaspoons hot syrup and work in well.

Take the syrup off the heat and fashion the nut paste into small walnut sized balls. Scatter the remaining pine nuts on a plate and dip a ball of nut paste briefly in the syrup. Lift it out with a fork and roll in the pine nuts so that it is well covered. Arrange on a plate and repeat, placing the balls so that they do not touch. Leave to dry for 24 hours before serving.

SWEET COUSCOUS

CUSCUSU DOLCE

Buying sweets at the convent of Santo Spirito in Agrigento, Sicily, I was astonished when the tiny nun behind her grille asked me whether I would also like some of their speciality, cuscusu. She disappeared for what seemed an age and finally returned proudly bearing a little dish of what did look like couscous, richly studded with nuts and dusted with cinnamon and icing sugar. 'A secret recipe we learnt from the Arabs,' she confided in me. 'It's really for Christmas but we like it so much we make some every week just for us nuns. Though it takes all night to make.' I didn't dare ask why it had to be made at night.

Later that day I ate the cuscusu on a hillside covered with wild flowers, looking over the snows of Mount Etna. It was so rich with pistachio and almonds that I couldn't detect any semolina grain. Further research in an old book on La cucina siculo-araba, which I had been given in Trapani revealed that the nuns of Agrigento have refined their cuscusu so much that indeed it does contain only nuts – the secret of their recipe. I can only assume that it took all night to chop the nuts in the quantities required.

100g (4oz) blanched almonds

100g (4oz) chopped blanched unsalted pistachios

100g (4oz) candied fruit, finely chopped

50g (2oz) icing sugar

1 teaspoon ground cinnamon

Finely chop the nuts so that they look like little grains of couscous. Mix in the chopped candied fruit and scatter over the icing sugar and cinnamon.

MARZIPAN SWEETS

Maysaban, *as it is called in Arabic, was a favourite way for the Moors to use the nuts of the almond trees they planted in al-Andaluz. However, not all stories credit them with the invention of this sweetened almond paste – there is a powerful tradition that marzipan was first created by the nuns of the Convent of San Clemente in the town of Toledo. Fighting between the Moors and Alfonso VIII of Castile in 1212 meant that supplies of flour were completely cut off so, the story goes, the nuns decided to use their large stocks of sugar and almonds to make a replacement, naming it after the* maza *or mallet used to crush the almonds and* pan *or bread.*

Whatever their origin, marzipan sweets are still made today in the convents of Spain and Portugal, often mixed with dried fruits and flavoured with a drop or two of rose-water. Meanwhile in Sicily the making of marzipan fruits has become a real art-form. The fruits are known as La Martorana, and the pasticcerie *of Palermo are filled with these elegant creations, imitating apricots blushed with pink or fresh green almonds, gorgeous fat peaches or spiky Barbary figs.*

There is no need to attempt such artistry but it is worth making your own marzipan – it is simple to do. The vanilla with which it is flavoured is a later import from the New World – for a truly Moorish flavour you can add a few drops of orange or rose-water.

200g (7oz) white sugar
1 vanilla pod
100ml (3½floz) water
200g (7oz) ground almonds

Put the sugar and vanilla pod in a small heavy pan over a low heat and add the water. Cook, stirring, for 5 minutes, until the syrup is clear and boiling. Remove the vanilla, rinse and save for another day.

Take the pan off the heat and slowly stir in the ground almonds. Return to the lowest possible heat and cook, stirring continuously, for 3 to 4 minutes, until the mixture is very thick and dry. On no account should it be allowed to take colour – if it looks like doing so lift the pan off the heat. Spread the paste out on greaseproof paper or aluminium foil and as soon as it is cool enough to handle mould into the required shapes. Leave to dry for a day before colouring with vegetable dye if desired.

ORANGE FLOWER BISCUITS

BISCUITS À L'EAU DE FLEUR D'ORANGER

2 large eggs
100g (4oz) white sugar
2 tablespoons orange flower water
225g (8oz) plain white flour

Preheat the oven to 220°C/425°F/gas mark 7.

Whisk together the eggs and the sugar then stir in the orange flower water. Slowly sift in the flour, stirring all the time with a wooden spoon, until you have a sticky dough. Dust the dough with flour and with your fingers fashion it into a cylinder about 5cm (2in) wide. Cut across the cylinder at 1.5cm (½in) intervals and place the biscuits on a buttered baking tray. Cook in the preheated oven for 10 minutes, until the biscuits just start to colour.

ALMOND AND CINNAMON BISCUITS

GRANADINAS

200g (7oz) butter, softened
400g (14oz) plain flour
2 large eggs
1 egg yolk
100g (4oz) ground almonds
200g (7oz) caster sugar
2 teaspoons ground cinnamon
¼ teaspoon ground mace or nutmeg

With your hands mix the butter into the flour until you have a fine crumble. Beat the whole eggs then stir them into the butter and flour mixture together with the remaining ingredients. Work well until you have a smooth dough. Wrap in clingfilm and chill in the fridge overnight.

When you are ready to bake the biscuits, preheat the oven to 200°C/400°F/gas mark 6.

Oil a baking sheet. On a well-floured surface, roll the pastry out to a thickness of 1.5cm (½in) and with a cutter or a small glass cut out rounds. Brush the surface of the biscuits with the egg yolk. Bake in the centre of the oven for 15 minutes, until lightly browned. Allow to cool before serving.

BUTTER BISCUITS

GHORIBA

These rich biscuits, which are favourites in Morocco, have an almost shortbread like quality. They are sometimes scented with orange flower water but I prefer to enjoy their buttery taste absolutely plain.

200 g (7 oz) unsalted butter

125 g (4½ oz) icing sugar

250 g (9 oz) plain flour

Whole blanched almonds or hazelnuts

Melt the butter and skim off the scum which rises to the surface. When the butter is cool but not yet set, mix in the sifted icing sugar. Slowly add the sifted flour, stirring all the time, until you have a smooth stiff dough. Work the dough as little as possible and place in the fridge for 15 minutes.

Preheat the oven to 180°C/350°F/gas mark 4.

Break off walnut sized pieces of dough and with lightly oiled hands mould them into round balls then gently press them flat. Place on a well-oiled baking sheet and press a whole nut of your choice into the centre. Continue until all the dough is used up, making sure you place the biscuits well apart – they spread during baking.

Bake in the pre-heated oven for 18 to 20 minutes, until golden and leave to cool before eating.

ICED LEMON DRINK

GRANIZADO DE LIMON

Granizado *is related to the Italian granita but instead of being served as a sorbet it takes the form of an icy drink – making it closer to the Arab* shar'bats. Granizados, *made with either orange or lemon juice, are particularly popular in the summer months in Majorca and Minorca.*

250g (9oz) white sugar

Zest of 1 lemon, preferably unwaxed

Juice of 4 lemons

750ml (1¼ pints) water

Mix together the sugar, lemon zest and water, bring to the boil and simmer for 2 minutes, until the sugar has dissolved. Stir in the lemon juice and leave to cool. Transfer to the freezer and freeze until slushy, beating with a fork every 30 minutes to break into crystals. Serve in tall glasses with a straw.

ALMOND MILK

HORCHATA

Now available commercially bottled and often made with the cheaper chufas *or tiger nuts, this popular Spanish drink is derived from the rich Moorish version based on almonds and has lent its name to the* horchaterias *which are found all over Spain but particularly around Valencia. Despite it's name, the drink contains no milk – the almonds infused in water give a milky colour and consistency instead. Well-chilled,* horchata *makes a refreshing and unusual summer drink.*

225g (8oz) ground almonds

1 litre (1¾ pints) water

1 cinnamon stick

50g (2oz) caster sugar

Mix together the sugar and water and bring to the boil, stirring continuously until the sugar dissolves. Take off the heat, add the cinnamon stick and leave to cool. When the liquid is quite cold, stir in the ground almonds and leave to stand for 24 hours. Strain and chill until on the verge of freezing before serving.

PRESERVES AND PICKLES

ABOVE: JARS OF PRESERVED FRUIT, RONDA, SPAIN. RIGHT: BLACK OLIVES FOR SALE IN LA VUCCIARIA, PALERMO, SICILY.

Food from Morocco and the southern Mediterranean gains much of its flavour and charm from the fact that cooks continue to follow the seasons. And where there is seasonality there will always be preserving and pickling in the kitchen, to ensure that the glut of the harvest or the slaughter can be spread over the year.

But in these days of freezers and 'global supply', the art of preserving no longer exists solely to ensure that seasonal produce is available all year round. Often the very process adds a distinctive flavour. So with the famous Moroccan lemons preserved in salt, which over a period of several months acquire a unique fragrance and sweetness; or the pickled aubergines of Almagro on the Spanish plain, which take just a week or two to absorb the powerful aromas of spices, garlic and vinegar.

In Morocco preserving is not confined to fruit and vegetables – when a sheep is slaughtered some of its meat will be preserved in fat for *k'hli*, still a favourite ingredient for family meals, whilst butter is salted and preserved for *smen*, also something of an acquired taste. But perhaps most famous of the preserves and pickles is *harissa*, the paste of dried chillies with spices without which no Tunisian or Algerian would consider a couscous complete. *Harissa* is however less commonly served in Morocco. On the other hand, no Moroccan table is complete without several bowls of olives, preserved in salt or brine and pickled in different herbs and spices.

Meanwhile in the southern Mediterranean the favourite preserves are made not with salt but with sugar, to be served at the end of the meal or with cheese, as in the quince paste of Spain. In Provence this art reached its pinnacle with the candied fruits of Avignon, which became so popular with the Popes. Quince, pumpkin, apricots, peaches, melons – all are still today preserved in the sweetness which the Moors first introduced.

PRESERVED SQUASH

MARMELLATA DI ZUCCA

Wherever they went the Moors planted sugar-cane and their legacy can be seen from the candied fruits of Avignon to the preserved squash of Sicily.

1 kg (2 lb) slice of pumpkin or other firm squash
250 g (9 oz) white sugar
150 ml (5 fl oz) water

Remove the pumpkin's skin and seeds and cut the flesh into strips 1 cm (½ in) wide. Mix the sugar and water and in a large wide pan, bring slowly to the boil, stirring all the time so that the sugar dissolves. Add the pumpkin strips, which should be in one layer. Simmer gently in the syrup for 45 minutes, stirring regularly to prevent the pumpkin sticking together, until the pumpkin is very soft and translucent.

Heat the oven to 110°C/225°F/gas mark ¼.

Lay the pumpkin strips on greaseproof paper on an oven tray, making sure none of them are touching. Bake in the oven overnight or for 8 hours. Leave to cool before putting in a sealed container.

PRESERVED QUINCE

1.5 kg (3 lb) quince
400 g (14 oz) white sugar
200 ml (7 fl oz) water
1 stick of cinnamon
Juice of ½ a lemon

Peel the quince and remove the core. Cut the hard flesh into sticks the thickness of your thumb. Choose a heavy pot or a preserving pan, place it over a low heat and add the water and the sugar. When the sugar has dissolved add the cinnamon stick, lemon juice and pieces of quince. Simmer the quince in the syrup for 30 minutes, until the fruit is tender. Do not allow the syrup to caramelize and brown. Bottle the quince in the sugar syrup and chill before serving.

MARINATED OLIVES

MESLALLA

There are many sights to delight the eye in a Moroccan souk but perhaps none more so than the olive sellers. Crammed into a tiny space behind their gleaming heaps of black, purple and green fruit, often so squeezed in that they have to use an overhead metal chain to swing out from behind their prizes or creep through a small door beneath their stall, they mix together blends of spices and herbs to flavour the olives.

Often three or four different kinds of olives will be served with the selection of salads at the beginning of the meal. This marinade of preserved lemon with the Moroccan trio of cumin, cayenne and paprika is my personal favourite.

300g (11oz) cracked green olives

Juice of 1 lemon

4 tablespoons olive oil

1 teaspoon ground cumin

1 teaspoon paprika

¼ teaspoon cayenne

1 preserved lemon, cut into thin strips

½ a bunch flat-leaf parsley, finely chopped

Rinse the olives in water and remove the stones. Mix the remaining ingredients into the olives and leave to marinate for 24 hours before serving with a selection of salads.

PRESERVED LEMONS

For me the preserved lemon is the defining taste of Moroccan cooking. It finds its way not just into tagines of lamb and chicken but into myriad salads as well, lending a unique blend of sourness and sweetness.

Preserved lemons are easy to make but they do require patience – I use mine after a month but the head chef at the Mammounia told me that theirs were left at least six months to mature. After this time the lemons turn a golden colour and their juice becomes thick, developing a honeyed sweetness over the sour flavour of salt and lemon and a soft texture which melts in the mouth.

The lemons should not be handled as this can taint them, but instead removed from the jar with a wooden spoon. And wherever possible try to use unwaxed lemons, so that you are not preserving chemicals. I once came back from Sicily with five kilos of lemons straight from the tree and made the best preserved lemons I had ever had. Finally, do not worry if the lemons at the top of the jar develop a white lacy covering – this is actually a good sign.

2 kg (4½ lb) lemons, preferably unwaxed

200 g (7 oz) coarse sea salt

Soak the lemons in water overnight. The next day quarter them from the top to within 1 cm (½ in) from the bottom, so that the lemons remain attached at one end. Sprinkle plenty of salt onto the cut flesh then reshape the lemons.

Place some salt on the base of a sterilized preserving jar, then pack in the lemons, sprinkling with salt as you go. Add the remaining salt and press down on the lemons to release their juices – there should be enough juice to cover the surface. If not, top up with additional fresh lemon juice.

Leave in a dark place for at least a month before using.

QUINCE PASTE

DULCE DE MEMBRILLO

The quince was one of the Moor's favourite fruit trees, planted in their courtyards to provide scent and shade. In 980 Shafer ben Utman al Mishafi, Vizir to the Second Caliph of Córdoba, even wrote a poem of love to the fruit. Quince was often cooked with meat in Persian-style but the introduction of sugar-cane also allowed the making of preserves and jams. Dulce de membrillo or quince paste remains very popular in Spain today, where it is traditionally served with a slice of Manchego cheese. I have also enjoyed in Andalucía quince preserved in sugar syrup, served ice cold at the end of the meal.

2 kg (2 lb) quinces
120 ml (4 fl oz) water
White sugar

Peel and core the quinces. Roughly chop the flesh and put it in a heavy pan with the water. Bring the water to the boil, turn down to a simmer, cover and leave to cook for 30 minutes. At the end of this time you will have a purée. Either process it or push it through a sieve to remove lumps. Weigh the purée and stir in 250 g (9 oz) of sugar per 500 g (1 lb) of pulp.

Return the sugared pulp to the pan and simmer for 45 minutes, uncovered. At the end of this time pour the mixture into a lightly greased oblong baking tray, to the depth of about 2.5 cm (1 in). Leave to cool and when it is completely cold cut into squares. Store in a tin wrapped in greaseproof paper.

HARISSA

This fiery red paste is always served with couscous in Tunisia and Algeria, where it is also often stirred into salads and cooked vegetable dishes to give a characteristic red colour. However it is found far less often in Morocco. It can be bought ready prepared, in tubes or jars, but it is worth the slight effort of making your own. The main issue is to find the right kind of peppers – you need large sweet but hot red chilli peppers which have been dried – I use ancho peppers.

Harissa is best made in small quantities but if you want to keep it for several days in the fridge float a little olive oil over the surface.

8 large dried red chilli peppers
Water
6 cloves garlic, peeled
1 teaspoon coarse sea salt
2 teaspoons ground coriander seeds
1 teaspoon ground cumin seeds

Remove the seeds and tops from the peppers and leave them to soak in just enough water to cover. Meanwhile crush the peeled garlic cloves with the salt. After 1 hour remove the peppers from the soaking liquid and process them with the garlic and salt to a slightly crunchy paste, adding just enough of the soaking water to achieve the right consistency. Stir in the spices and refrigerate.

AUBERGINES ALMAGRO STYLE
BERENJAS DE ALMAGRO

On the plains of La Mancha, south of Ciudad Real, lies the strange town of Almagro, Spanish home to the German banking family, the Fuggers. Their influence shows in the most un-Spanish homogeneity and perfectionism of the main square and in the lace-making for which Almagro is famous. More interestingly to me, it is also renowned for its pickled aubergines, favourite vegetable of the Moors, who took a tolerant view of wine in Spain and often used vinegar for preserving. Similar versions of this pickle are also found in Sicily and Tunisia.

750g (1½lb) small aubergines

Sea salt

4 tablespoons red wine vinegar

4 tablespoons olive oil

¾ teaspoon ground cumin

¼ teaspoon cayenne pepper

½ teaspoon paprika

2 cloves garlic, minced

¼ teaspoon dried oregano

Cut the aubergines in half lengthways, leaving the stalks intact. Bring a large pan of salted water to the boil and cook the aubergines for 8 minutes, until just tender. Drain, leave to cool slightly then pack into a sterilized preserving jar.

Mix together the remaining ingredients and pour over the aubergines. If the liquid does not quite cover them, add a little water to do so. Seal and leave for a week before eating.

INDEX